Normal
The Supernatural Life you were Created to Live

Normal
The Supernatural Life you were Created to Live

Gene Lloyd

Normal

Expanded Edition

Copyright © 2014, 2017 by Gene Lloyd

www.nomorewounds.org
ministry@nomorewounds.org
facebook.com/woundednomore
@genelloyd

All quotations taken from the Holy Bible, New International Version. Copyright © 1973, 1984 by international Bible Society. Used by permission.

Scripture quotations taken from the New American Standard Bible®, Copyright © 1960, 1962, 1963, 1968, 1971, 1972, 1973, 1975, 1977, 1995 by The Lockman Foundation
Used by permission.

Published in the United States by
WNM Publishing
Alexandria, VA

Printed in the Unites States of America

ALL RIGHTS RESERVED

No part of this publication may be reproduced, stored in a retrieval system, or transmitted in any form, or by any means-electronic, mechanical, photocopying, recording, scanning, or other-except for brief quotations in critical reviews, or articles without prior written permission.

First Printing: June 2014

Expanded Edition: December 2017

Library of Congress Cataloging-in-Publication Data

Lloyd, Gene.

Normal / Gene Lloyd.

ISBN: 0692049428
ISBN-13: 978-0692049426

ACKNOWLEDGEMENTS

Thank you so much to my wife, Lauren, whose constant love, support, and affirmation makes everything I do so much more exciting and enjoyable. I love you more now than the day we met. I also want to thank all the leaders who have spoken into my life over the years. Your leadership has spurred me forward into a lifestyle I never dreamed possible, and I am happy to be numbered as a fruit of your ministry.

CONTENTS

Acknowledgements		
Introduction		11
Chapter 1	My Story	14
Chapter 2	Identity	27
Chapter 3	Fully Paid	42
Chapter 4	Partners	55
Chapter 5	Act Like A Kid	68
Chapter 6	Risk	81
Chapter 7	Mandate	94
Chapter 8	Addiction	108
Chapter 9	Presence	122
Chapter 10	Angels	136
Chapter 11	Getting Started	150
Chapter 12	Testimonies	166
Epilogue		176
Impartation		187

INTRODUCTION

I see miracles happen every week. I'm not talking about the miracle of waking up, or the miracle of seeing the sun rise. I see actual miracles. I see people miraculously healed. You could even say that miracles chase me. I see bones instantaneously grow, mobility restored, muscles stitched back together, pain leave, eyes opened, headaches dissipate, and so much more. I'm not a doctor. I'm a follower of Jesus. And I have learned how to access what God has available for anyone who is willing to take hold of it. In John 14[1] Jesus said, "whoever believes in me will do the works I have been doing, and they will do even greater things than these." So, at the very least we should be doing what Jesus did; healing the sick, sharing the good news, raising the dead, dispatching demons, and restoring the outcasts of society. Now this doesn't mean you should be standing on the street corner with a megaphone screaming at all the people within ear shot. It's all about love. And when you love people the way Jesus loves them you can't avoid doing the things Jesus did. But he also said that we would do greater things than he did while he was on the earth. That is a powerful statement; what is greater than raising the dead, or walking on water? I propose the point was not that the individual miracles would be greater, but that the number of miracles would be greater because there would be more people involved in bringing those miracles to the masses. The "more people" are you and me operating in the gifts of the Holy Spirit that God has made available to us. The disciples were told in Luke 24 to "stay in the city until you have been clothed with power from on high," and then there was an explosion of miracles through them after the upper room experience a few days later.

There are times when I intentionally look for sick people everywhere I go. It didn't used to be that way, but it's something I am growing into. I don't actually have the power to heal anyone, but I have come to realize that there is so much more of God available to anyone who believes, and all it takes to get started down the path towards a lifestyle of miracles is a little bit of faith. Healing the sick is not just for the super anointed, it is for everyone. It should be normal for every Christian to see supernatural events occurring in, and around them. I do think that some are given special anointing's because they have been chosen by God to play a larger role, but that does not negate the authority every Christian has to access what God has made available. This book has only one purpose; to change your definition of normal so that it includes supernatural events. The simple fact is that most Christians do not know what they believe. Or at the very least they don't know what being a follower of Christ is all about. The basics of going to church, reading your Bible, and being a generally good person are pretty easy, but following Christ is so much more than that. This book is not a diatribe about all the things Christians are doing wrong, but rather it is a look at some major elements of Jesus' teaching that, if implemented as part of a normal Christian lifestyle, would dramatically change the landscape of not just the Church, but the entire world. I guarantee that, if you step out in faith, you will start seeing miracles by the time you finish reading this book. God has called us to do so much more than sit inside the four walls of a building. We live in a hurting world, and we have access to the cure to make everything better. My prayer is that God will allow you to touch his heart, and feel his love for the people around you. My hope is that as you read the pages of this book you will be inspired to go do more.

Endnotes
1. John 14:12

CHAPTER ONE

MY STORY

If you met me ten years ago you would have found a guy who was pretty happy with his situation in life. My wife and I had a nice house, good jobs, and went to a good church. The only problem is that I was comfortable; a little too comfortable. It wasn't until we moved to the East coast that I realized I had been living on a plateau. I became so comfortable that I stopped growing in my faith, and as I look back at that time I can easily recognize the danger of ending up on one of these plateau's. Unfortunately a lot of Christians are in that same position, and it's an easy one to get into. We get wrapped up in our lives, and going to church becomes just another routine. It's something that affects all of us; even pastors get caught up in the trap of a comfortable, stable congregation with a regular inflow of tithes, and a fairly easy routine of preaching to the choir a few times each week. I was more involved in ministry than the average person, and spent quite a lot of time working with teenagers, but even that just became another routine. I had lost my hunger, and the worst part of this story is that I didn't even know it. I think that is the same of everyone in that situation. You think you are doing pretty well because you're at church several times each week, reading your Bible, and praying every day; doing all the stuff a good Christian is supposed to do. But like where I ended up, there's a good chance any other believer can end up on a plateau. The way I see it is that the problem stems from Christians not knowing everything there is to know about their faith. There's a lot that doesn't get discussed in churches for a variety of reasons that we don't need to go into here, but the point is that the church isn't doing all it could to equip the saints. It's time to fill the ever widening gap that is prohibiting the equipping of God's army.

But first you need the backstory, so here we go. I grew up the son of a part-time evangelist who, during my younger years, was often used by God in miraculous ways. Dad was old school. He would setup a big circus tent on a dirt lot, and then launch into a weeklong church service where people would be healed of a variety of sicknesses. Blind eyes would see again, deaf ears would be opened, the crippled would walk, and the list goes on. I was pretty young during the height of his ministry, but there has been a lasting impact from the things I saw, and experienced; seeing miracles became a normal part of a portion of my childhood. That's an interesting comment to make, and probably even more interesting to read. When you sit in an old metal folding chair on a dirt lot under a tent, and curiously watch as someone gets out of a wheel chair, and starts walking, it impacts your way of thinking. Seeing miracles is exciting enough, but as a kid they take on a different meaning. When you're young, and impressionable the experiences you have make a more lasting impact than the ones later in life. I guess at some point I began to think that miracles were normal. That's probably not unusual for the environment I was in. I suppose a kid growing up in an, orphanage with very little food available would eventually come to the assumption that it was normal to not have a lot of food. You see, we're colored by our environments, and our experiences. My environment had some amazing supernatural elements weaved into it that shaped the way I think today.

My dad suffered a series of strokes in his 50's that left him in a pretty bad state. It seems like he aged 20 years over night, and at times he lost his ability to function as a normal adult. During this season, I went back home for a visit, and while we were out shopping one day, my mom mentioned she didn't feel well; Dad instinctively prayed, and mom got better. After seeing what happened I said "hey dad you still got it," and he simply replied "no, God is just merciful." Even in an injured state, his faith in God to perform miracles was still intact, and his understanding that it had nothing to do with him was profoundly moving. It was the first miracle I remember seeing since I was a kid, and I wasn't even surprised because it seemed perfectly normal that dad saw a need, and was able to pull resources from heaven to provide a solution. What was more interesting to me about this event is that dad hadn't been actively ministering in quite some time. Having six kids to provide for pushed him more into becoming a businessman, and away from preaching. Compile that with a handful of strokes, and you would think he wouldn't have much impact on supernatural events. I guess that shows that God's mercy has nothing to do with us.

It was those early childhood events that convinced me God was real, and that created an anchor point for my adolescent, and young adult years. Even though I stayed in church, and jumped into part-time ministry myself, for some reason I never pursued a miraculous lifestyle. I knew God could, and still did heal people, but it wasn't something I was focused on. Maybe I thought that type of lifestyle was only available to a select few, or maybe it just wasn't something that interested me. Whatever the reason, it was a pursuit that I didn't take. Seeing miracles as a kid certainly created a faith in me that I now realize impacts me more today than it ever did throughout my life. But when you end up on a plateau as I did, faith doesn't take up much space in your life. Somewhere along the way I found my hunger again. Somewhere along the way I realized God had more for me, and I wanted it. I remembered earlier times in my life where people told me God was going to use me in powerful ways, and those words started to become important to me again. It was then I realized that even though God had a big plan for my life he wasn't just going to drop it into my lap. I had to pursue it. I had to pursue Him. This was the turning point for me to get off of cruise control, and get back in the game. It might seem a little strange that you could be involved in ministry, and be on cruise control at the same time, but I think this is probably the case in many churches around the world. Being comfortable is a liability, and I'm happy God reignited the flame in my heart.

One summer, in the middle of June, while traveling on my last official trip for the Air Force, I was praying in my hotel room when suddenly electricity began to surround, and flow through my hands. This wasn't the first time I experienced this, but it was different from what I had felt before. Several years earlier, I had felt a similar sensation while worshipping during a Saturday night service at the church I attended in San Antonio. I lifted my hands, and began to feel a tingling sensation as if my hands had fallen asleep. I put them back down, and it went away. I thought that was interesting, so out of curiosity, I lifted them again, and the sensation came back. I knew God was up to something, but I had no grid for what was happening. My interest was definitely piqued, and I experimented for the next few minutes to try, and figure out what was happening. I shared the experience with my wife when we went home that afternoon, but neither of us really knew what it meant. The following week we returned to church, and it happened again in the same way. This went on for a few weeks, and then, it just stopped. As I look back now I think my problem then was that I didn't thank God for what he was doing, or even really inquire about what was going on. I was curious for sure, but not curious enough to pursue, or steward it, and so it seemed that God stopped. I now realize that God was trying to get my attention because he wanted to do something new in my life, but I was comfortable where I was, so he had to shake some other things loose before he continued. But that's another story for another time, let's get back to the hotel room.

When I began to pray in that hotel room I asked the Lord to restart what he had begun a few years earlier. I wanted to feel that electricity again, and this time I didn't want it to ever go away. But it was about more than just feeling electricity. It was about drawing closer to him, and pursuing a deeper relationship with the one who gave everything for me. I didn't know what that would cost me at the time, but I was willing to give up anything to have him. I asked that he would let me feel his presence every moment of every day. I never again wanted to be outside of his presence. I never wanted to have a single moment where I didn't feel him in some way because I knew that if I could stay in his presence then it would carry my relationship with him to a much deeper level. There's this great verse in 2 Chronicles[1] that talks about God lending his strength to those who are committed to him, and I wanted this verse to apply to me.

My desire was that when God searched the earth he would spot me, and would be attracted to the living sacrifice that I was offering up for his use. I decided at that point that I was going to live in such a way that his presence would be attracted to me. When God's eyes roam the earth I want him to stop, and stare when he gets to me. Never out of his presence had become my new goal. I have been a believer since I was very young, and I have understood the importance of maintaining a relationship with him, but I don't think I realized how serious God was about cultivating the relationship with me. He was chasing me, and he caught me that night in June. But now the roles have been reversed, and I have the pleasure of chasing him! There I was in the hotel room, and when this electricity hit my hands, I became so excited that it was back, that my approach to God from that point forward has been out of an abundance of thankfulness for what he is continuously doing in my life. The experiences intensified over the next several months as the electricity began to spread until it eventually covered my entire body while lying in bed one night.

While praying in my living room a few days after returning home I noticed my feet had become electrified in addition to my hands. A few days later it was on my calves as well. I asked the Lord what he was doing, and his response was as enlightening as it was simple. "Why my legs Lord?" "Why my feet?" And he responded by telling me that he fills a cup from the bottom up, not the top down. And it continued for several months. I would wake up in the morning, and my hands would be full of power. I would walk down the halls of work, and I would feel it. Interestingly enough, one day I was walking through the Pentagon, down the hallway where the offices of Joint Chiefs of Staff were located, and right about the time I passed the Chairman's office, I began to feel electricity on my arms, and hands a little more intensely than before. I thought it was an odd place for a new touch, but then God showed me that a lot of spiritual activity happens around places of great authority on earth. I suppose that could mean good, or evil activity depending on the location, or people involved, but in this case it may have just been an opportunity for God to teach me something. Or maybe I just bumped into an angel. Who knows? Anyways, the electricity continued to migrate over the next few months onto my back, neck, head, face, and even on my ears, and eyes. The intensity, or amount of current increased from time to time, but never to the point that Bill Johnson, and Randy Clark describe as being painfully powerful in one of their books[2]. Instead of being a mass amount of power all at once, it was spurts of power all the time. Everywhere I went I would feel electricity in various spots of my body, and it was almost continuous throughout each day. Early one morning in October of the same year while I was praying the Lord told me he was going to change the electricity into something else, but that I shouldn't be concerned because he wasn't withdrawing from me. I don't know why he put that last part in there except that maybe he knew I would be concerned about losing something he had given me. But I'm happy he made the change because what came next was even better.

Before I discuss the change I want to first share a few other interesting experiences I had during that four month period. One Saturday evening during the worship service at church I felt someone walk past me, but when I opened my eyes no one was moving around. I'm certain someone walked past as I could feel the air shift around me, and it's the first time I remember feeling this sensation in our church. An angel was the only explanation I could come up with though, I suppose it could have been one of those other things, but we won't worry about that right now. Later that night while praying, I began to feel something on my left shoulder. At first, I thought it felt like someone was brushing my shoulder with a feather. There wasn't anyone else in the room, so my mind began to race through the various possibilities. Is there an angel in the room? Did an angel's wing brush up against me? This was all new territory for me. Feeling electricity became normal by this point, and I was excited about anything new God gave me, but I didn't have a barometer to test what was happening. A few days later the Lord revealed to me that the sensation on my shoulder was a small flame. It was then that I realized I could feel this flame flicker as the air moved around me. I couldn't see anything, and there wasn't any heat coming from it, but I could certainly feel it. This happened off, and on for a few days, and also began to spread to other parts of my body. Eventually I felt it across my shoulders, and on my hands. I even felt it on my toes a few times. There's probably a good athlete's foot joke in there somewhere; burning feet, and all. I have found through these experiences that we know very little about God, and even less about how he works. I have also found that what makes this chase so fun is the new discoveries that keep popping up. The more we pursue, the more there is to discover, and there is an endless supply of discoveries waiting for everyone who is willing to take this pursuit seriously.

Now, back to the change I mentioned. In October of the same year my wife and I drove up to Lancaster, Pennsylvania to attend the Voice of the Apostles conference. I should probably note at this point that when this new experience of God's outpouring began, I had been watching sermons on the Bethel Redding website over the preceding few days. The messages were so impactful that I knew I needed to learn more from the speakers at this event, or similar speakers. It really began to birth a hunger within me, so it was in that same timeframe that I reserved a hotel in Lancaster, and purchased our tickets to attend this conference. Part of me feels like God moved because I decided to make a commitment to go wherever he was moving. In this case, I knew he would be in Lancaster because highly anointed people would be there. And I knew he was a regular attendee in the services at Bethel because of all of the miracles happening in that place. So if the pastor of Bethel is going to be at a conference a one hundred miles north of my home, I'm going! And if the missionaries to Mozambique who see dead people come back to life are going to be at a conference one hundred miles north of my home, I'm going! And if the guy who God has used to heal thousands of people all over the world is going to be at a conference one hundred miles north of my home, I'm going! You get the point. Let me be clear; I wasn't going to a conference as a groupie who wanted to see a couple of famous people. There were certainly a lot of people there with that mindset, but I was going because I wanted to have an encounter with God. I committed to go where I knew God would be moving, and then, God began to move on me. So when I showed up for the Wednesday night service that week I came with a lot of expectation.

At some point during the service that first night my neck got really hot. It felt like I was standing just a little too close to a campfire; lots of heat accompanied by a little bit of pain. And that has become a common occurrence for me since that night. God answered my earlier prayers, and now he allows me to feel his manifest presence on an almost continuous basis. As we went back to the hotel room that night my neck was still on fire, and it stayed that way through the night, and on into the next day. During the second day of the conference, Randy Clark had a time of impartation, and while I was praying, I felt like someone had poured a hot liquid over my head, and shoulders. A few moments later I felt a hand on my chest, but when I opened my eyes there wasn't anyone standing in front of me. My wife had some similar experiences during the same service, and I have no doubt that the Lord sent an angel to commission us. She was just as hungry as I was, if not hungrier, and I know that our hunger attracted his presence in a way that has permanently marked out lives. During these times of outpouring I had asked the Lord to give her what he has given to me, and vice versa. I wanted us to be able to experience these outpourings together. It seems that our combined pursuit of more brought about a similar anointing, and spiritual gifts for both of us that now allows us to minister as a team, experience many of the same things in God's presence, and see many lives transformed as a result. During the week of the conference, the manifestations of electricity went away for a season, and was replaced by heat, just as the Lord had told me would happen, and that heat continues to be a normal part of our lives today with intense increase during times of prayer, or ministry.

I have felt this heat all over my body as I did the electricity, and it usually shows up on my neck, chest, and hands. But occasionally I also feel it in my legs, and feet. One particular night I asked the Lord for more, and I specifically said I didn't even care if it caused pain. That seems like a strange thing to say, but something I learned along the way is that powerful touches from God are often accompanied by some form of uncomfortableness. That was an uncomfortable night because as I lay in bed my chest was on fire. It hurt, but I kept asking for more. The next morning the skin in the center of my chest was very dry, and it took a few weeks of applying lotion to get it back to normal. At other times my neck would look a little splotchy as if I had a rash. And my palms will also take on a splotchy appearance, and get hot as the anointing increased. It became an everyday experience that I will not trade for anything, and that I do not ever want to lose, so I try to live with the constant awareness of the presence of the Holy Spirit resting upon me. One thing I have learned is that it is incredibly important to steward what God gives you. In the parable of the talents in Matthew 25[3] we see that the servants who invested the boss's money were rewarded while the one who hid what he was given was punished. God wants us to manage, and spend what he gives us because the gifts are meant for us to give away. When it comes to stewarding his presence I have developed a habit of not getting out of bed in the morning until I invite him to come. I told the Lord that getting out of bed is pointless if he isn't with me. I have no desire to do anything if his anointing isn't present upon me. So when I wake up every morning my first action is to sit up in bed, and invite the Holy Spirit to come. When I first started doing this it would take a minute of pressing in before I felt the Lord's presence, but now I often feel the Holy Spirit hovering over the bed as I wake up.

The curious thing to me, and the one thing I pondered for some time was that we didn't immediately start seeing any miraculous healings after the experience in Lancaster. I wondered how I could be so blessed with God's presence without seeing any fruit. Hosting the presence is certainly miraculous in, and of itself, but I wanted to see more. I felt like the Lord said I was in a season of training, so I just started praying for anyone who I could at church services, or other church events. People would tell me that they felt electricity, or heat when I prayed for them, and I waited with great anticipation for what the Lord was going to do next. Since that time we have seen hundreds of people healed, and the miracles are now occurring as often as we have opportunities to pray for the sick. I mentioned earlier that throughout my life there have been times that various people have spoken prophetic words over me, or my wife about the great things God would do with us, and through us. The funny thing about this is that most of those earlier prophecies were given to others about us. People we never met, even to this day as far as I know, were telling relatives that God was going to use us. In one particular instance in 1995 when a prophetic word was given directly to me, I was told that God and I together were going to make a tremendous team. I have stewarded that over the years, and kept a copy of the words given to me that night in my journal waiting for the day when tremendous things would begin to happen. I have also always pondered what it would be, and how it would start. Well, now I know at least part of the answer to that question, and I look forward to the mystery of what he will do next. Part of the thrill of the chase is trying to figure out the mystery.

I'm sharing these experiences in this first chapter because I want you to know that God has more for you, and he wants to use you in amazing ways. God can, and will use anyone, and if you are willing to passionately pursue him, you will catch him. Jacob wrestled with God in Genesis 32[4], and received a blessing afterwards. He refused to let go until he received a blessing. There's a powerful lesson in that story. God likes it when we pursue encounters with him, and he enjoys showing up with a blessing for us. The rest of this book is about the supernatural life you as a Christian can, and should be living. It's uncharted territory for most believers because there has been a lack of training within the church walls. Many don't understand how to operate in the spiritual gifts, so they simply ignore that area of Christianity. I'm here to get you trained up so you can get out on the streets, and help God change the world. Every day of my life is a new adventure of discovering God, and if you are willing to take some risk, every day of your life can be the same.

Endnotes
1. 2 Chronicles 16:9
2. There's more about this in Healing Unplugged: Conversations, and Insights from Two Veteran Healing Leaders by Bill Johnson, and Randy Clark
3. Matthew 25:14-30
4. Genesis 32:24

Going Deeper

1. Do you find yourself in a place of being too comfortable in your walk with Jesus right now?

---

2. What is one step you could make today that will draw you closer to God's presence?

---

3. How much are you willing to sacrifice to have everything God planned for your life?

---

4. What, if anything, is holding you back?

Deeper Prayer

If you are hungry for more, I invite you to pray this prayer:

Father God, my desire is to be closer to you, to encounter your presence in the same way mentioned throughout the bible, to clearly hear your voice speaking to me, and to know you as a friend. I want to see the world transformed by your love, and I want to partner with you, so that I can carry the change that the world needs. Use me for your glory. Use me for your purposes. Use me for your will. I will go anywhere, and do anything you call me to do. All I ask in return is for more of you. Let your presence go with me, surround me, and flow through me with the power, and authority to transform lives so that your kingdom can be fully established on the earth. I commit myself fully to your cause, and I am ready to go to a whole new level with you.

CHAPTER TWO

IDENTITY

A great series of movies came out in the late 1990's, and early 2000's that had a plot line which primarily focused on the identity of one of its main characters; the whole focus was on whether, or not this one character, Neo, was the one they thought would save the world, and win the war. The Matrix trilogy started with a character that had no clue about who he was, or the world he lived in. Neo was living out what he thought was a normal lifestyle until he encountered someone who revealed a greater truth to him, and opened his eyes to the reality of his true identity. Many Christians walk a similar path of not knowing who they are, or the reality of their purpose on earth. They haven't been introduced to, or embraced, their true identity. Here's what happens; we grow up being told "this is who you are," and then we attach that label to ourselves for the rest of our lives. Sometimes that label is about our race, or about the color of our skin. Sometimes it's attached to where we grew up, or the financial status of our family. And sometimes it comes from the words people have spoken over us.

We crave identity. We crave individuality. We crave to be celebrated for our diversity, and uniqueness. So we latch onto these other identities that people have labeled us with, and in the process end up missing out on who God says we are. And once we grab onto an identity, it is incredibly hard to lay it down. This is why it is so difficult to minister to people who have absorbed a false identity as their own. Telling someone that the lifestyle they choose to live is not who they were created to be can easily illicit an angry response because it can be viewed as an attack on what they perceive to be their identity. One example of this is the homosexual lifestyle where people have grabbed hold of an identity that is completely opposite of God's creative plan for their life. At some point in time, the notion surfaced that people can be born homosexual, so some have attached that label to themselves, and until they know their true identity, they won't be able to lay it down. Racism is another great example of people who have adopted a false identity of believing their stature is higher than others simply because of the color of their skin. These identity labels can come from what others speak over us, or from what we believe about ourselves. Some are healthy, some are unhealthy, and they can pop up almost anywhere.

I spent 20 years in the military where identity is often attached to the rank you wear on your uniform. New military members are given a lot of responsibility, and authority early on as they are handed big guns, and sent off to fight on battlefields, or protect national level resources. But those same people are often spoken to in disparaging ways because of their lower rank. The military culture cultivates the notion that people in the lower rank echelons are less important than those holding higher ranks. This can affect a young military member's identity, making them think that their lives are not as valuable as others while still in a critical development stage of their life. This is why it is so important to speak God's words into people's lives, so they can grow into their true identity. During my military career, I carried a military ID card everywhere I went. This card gave me access to a slew of resources that non-military members couldn't access. I had access to military bases all over the world, free medical care at any hospital in the United States, and many more overseas. I had the ability to shop in restricted stores, this card acted as a passport when I traveled on military, orders, and the list goes on. I was even lucky enough to get out of a few minor traffic tickets when the policeman realized my military affiliation. This card identified me as a member of a club, and as a member I had access to all the privileges of that club. We all end up carrying a handful of different identities through our lives as we graduate schools, accept jobs, and join different, organizations. Each identity entitles us to the privileges associated with the position we hold, and when you join this club we call Christianity you are given yet another identity, but this one is a little different. You don't get a gold plated ID card with a shiny picture. Nor do you carry a note in your wallet, or purse that identifies you as a friend of God. But you do get an identity. This is one of the most misunderstood areas of Christianity, so pay close attention. When you become a Christian you receive a new identity that grants you unlimited access to everything Jesus has. Let me say that again a different way; when you become a Christian you receive the authority to reach up into heaven, and pull down anything you need for yourself, or others. Now that's a pretty bold statement, so I'll need to unpack it a bit, but before I do, let me share another bold statement with you.

Your identity in Christ allows you to represent him in exactly the same way he walked on earth. Jesus healed the sick everywhere he went. He cancelled the assignments of demons, and sent them packing. And he turned funerals into celebrations by raising the dead back to life. In Matthew 10[1] he told the disciples to heal the sick, raise the dead, cleanse the lepers, and drive out demons. And again in Luke 10[2] he commissioned another 72 disciples to continue doing what he had started. It wasn't just a mandate for the, original 12, nor was it only for the 72 that followed. It is a mandate for every disciple of Jesus, and that includes you. Your identity gives you authority, and responsibility; let me show you some of what the Bible says about your identity.

You are the light of the world[3]

I remember as a kid singing a silly song that said "this little light of mine, I'm gonna let it shine…" as we learned that Jesus' light shines through us. I have come to realize that this song is completely inaccurate. To be a little gruffer, that song is a complete lie! When I think of the light of the world the first thought that comes to mind is, of course, Jesus, and my second thought is the sun in the sky. There is nothing little about the light I carry, and you don't carry a little light either. Jesus is the brightest light in the universe, and He is shining through you. You carry a blazing sun that cannot ever be covered up, or blotted out. Think about the brightness of the sun for a minute. It cuts through almost 93 million miles of darkness to provide warmth, and light for the entire planet. You can't be in the same room with the sun, and be in darkness at the same time. It's not possible. If believers are truly the light of the world, as Jesus said, then when we show up in a dark place, the darkness has to run. It's just like flipping on a light switch in a dark room. The darkness doesn't get to ask permission if it can stay. It has to leave as soon as the light turns on. So, when you walk into a room, what should happen? Darkness should run! No matter how evil an area might seem to others, when you show up, it is full of light. Darkness is actually defined as the absence of light. When light shows up, darkness leaves, and when you learn to walk from that perspective, demons will literally freak out when you show up. It happened to Jesus when he met the demonized man at the tombs. The demons didn't put up a fight at all. It was actually quite the opposite. They begged to not be tortured, and asked for permission to go hang out with a herd of pigs. The light showed up, and the darkness couldn't get away fast enough.

I was on a subway train one day, on my way home from work, when I noticed a group of local students were on the same car as me. After observing them for a few minutes I suspected some of them had some spiritual problems, so I decided to conduct a little experiment. I theorized that if there were any demonic spirits influencing the students, releasing a little light would flush them out. Demons like to stay hidden, but when the light of the world shows up they can't stay hidden anymore. Remember, darkness runs from the light, so I decided to quietly invite the presence of God onto the train, and what happened next was very interesting. Most of the students continued to sit quietly, but a few of them immediately became disruptive. One young lady became very agitated, and began repeating over, and over in a loud voice that she wanted to go home. Another began to stare at me with an extremely evil look, and a third began wringing his hands together with an intense nervousness. What struck me as the most interesting is that all three of them knew where the light was coming from. I don't think they understood from a physical perspective, but the spirit that was on them definitely knew what was happening. Now, I probably didn't take the best approach as it created a bit of a scene on the train car until the students left a few stops later. And the teachers probably had their hands full for the rest of the day. Luckily the train car was mostly empty. But the experiment was a success. When I turned on the light the enemy could no longer hide, and they didn't like that.

There have been other times where just being in an area has caused a stir in the spiritual realm that brought about a little disruptive behavior from people who were being influenced by evil spirits. We visited a neighborhood one day to look at a building that we were considering renting for an event. While we were waiting on the street corner, we noticed a man walking along the opposite side of the street who, when he saw us, began to glare at us with intense anger. We have received these types of stares plenty of times, so that didn't faze us, but then the man decided to walk across the street, through traffic, while yelling obscenities at us. He even tried to punch someone riding by on a bicycle because the rider didn't get out of his way. He then stood in front of us, and asked, in an intimidating way, "what is your intention here?" This reminded me of the encounters Jesus often had with the demonic when they would question why he was in their area. We knew this wasn't the man speaking to us, but rather, the spirit inside of him. But we also knew that it wasn't the appropriate time, or place to command the spirit to leave. We told him that we were there to bless the neighborhood. He didn't like that at all. He started to declare curses over the neighborhood, and over the church building on the corner, all the while becoming more angry. I think the goal was to try to intimidate us, but we simply told him his curses had no power, and after a few minutes he decided to leave. Welcome to our life. This type of activity has become more common as we continue to pursue more of God, and I actually find it a little comical because it shows me that we are doing something right if the enemy gets scared when we show up.

You are the salt of the earth[4]

I like salt. It makes a lot of food taste better. Some even say that salt makes everything taste better. I like it on watermelon, I like it in a good salsa, I like it on barbeque; in fact I don't think there is too much food that salt doesn't affect in a positive way. In the same way salt makes food taste better, we, as the salt of the earth, have the potential to make the earth better. We bring another element to the mix that makes it more exciting, that makes life pop the way salt makes food pop. We have the ability, and the mandate, to season the sea of humanity into a flavorful mix of God's amazing design. Jesus even mentioned in Matthew 5 that the salt is useless if it loses its flavor. And that is the position some believers, and churches are in today. They have become bland, and boring with no real seasoning happening in their ministry. I think that the world does not look to the church for help because they see it as a flavorless religious institution instead of a supernatural powerhouse. What makes salt effective is when you mix it into the food instead of just sprinkling it onto the surface. It needs to be rubbed into the meat before it is put on the grill if you want to get the full effect. We can't just drop a church in the middle of the neighborhood, and expect our saltiness to do any good. We have to rub it into the streets, the corporate workplaces, the restaurants, the airports, and anywhere else people go. You are the salt of the earth, and when you release God's presence it's like rubbing a seasoning into the atmosphere around you. You literally have the opportunity to make anything better. And unlike food, there is no such thing as spreading too much. Ask God to show you how you can be more intentional about being the salt of the earth, and then, go pour it out everywhere you can, and every chance you get.

You are seated with Christ in heavenly places[5]

Imagine for a moment that you are standing in the throne room of God. Picture Jesus sitting on his throne, and then pan just a little to the side, and picture yourself sitting on a chair right next to his throne. How does that feel? Seated next to Christ; sitting on a chair next to the creator of the universe. But wait a minute. Ephesians 2:6 doesn't say you are seated next to him, it says you are seated with him. So toss the folding chair out of your imagination, and climb up on the throne. With over two billion Christians on the planet that throne is going to get a little crowded, but don't worry, there's plenty of room for everyone. Does it feel good to know that your position with God is not one where you are billions of miles away on a planet in a distant galaxy? Your position is with him. When you pray, your prayers don't have to traverse space, and time, they simply go from your lips to his ears in an instant, and there is never a question as to whether, or not he heard you pouring out your heart. But it's more than just a proximity that allows you to converse. Your place with him affords you the opportunity to touch his heart, to learn to love what he loves, and to feel the compassion he has for his creation. Your place is a place of rest where you can soak in his presence, and then take what you have received, and release it to others. When you're having a tough day at school, or you get frustrated with your job all you have to do is remember you are seated with Christ in the heavenlies; that's a pretty powerful place to be.

Everything Jesus paid for is your inheritance[6]

I'll share some thoughts in the next chapter with more details on what exactly Jesus paid for, but for now, let's just hit the broad strokes of what this means. Everything Jesus paid for is available to you. When we think of the cross we tend to immediately think of salvation because that's the major thing that Jesus paid for, but there is actually so much more to the equation. He also paid for your physical healing, so you don't have to go through life with pain, he paid for your freedom, so you can be delivered from spiritual bondage, and his death paved the way to fill your life with peace, joy, and love. Being a Christian isn't just about getting a ticket to heaven; it's about inheriting all of God's goodness, and spreading that inheritance across the earth. The key here is that you are supposed to share the wealth. I wouldn't be a very good Christian if I kept everything the Lord taught me to myself. Sure, I can go get people healed, and delivered, but if I don't teach others how to do the same thing, I am not properly stewarding this inheritance. Think of yourselves as royalty, as sons, and daughters of The King of all kings. You are seated in the heavenlies, but you are not a beggar hoping the king tosses something your way. Nor are you a slave trudging away on menial tasks in the king's court. Jesus' death gave you access to everything he has, and that level of access comes with the amazing privilege of sharing the inheritance with everyone else. And there is always more than enough for everyone.

You are a friend of God[7]

Jesus had this interesting conversation with the disciples in John 15 as he discussed with them the difference between being a servant, and being a friend. Earlier on in the first chapter of this same book we are given the title of children of God. But in this passage Jesus shows us that the relationship with the disciples, and with us by extension, has been elevated from that of a slave, or servant to that of a friend. This was a serious promotion! Servants don't have the same level of access to their master as a friends do. Friends get to sit around the campfire, and fry fish with Jesus. Friends get to ask the tough questions about life like "why do disasters happen?", or "why is it taking so long for the Spurs to win another championship?" We're not relegated to the back seats, or cursory hellos. We're friends with the dude who can do anything. But the interesting thing here is that we're not just calling him our friend, he is calling us his friend. It's one thing for me to say "I'm friends with Jesus," but it is something entirely different when Jesus says "I'm friends with Gene." It's amazing to think about the reality that he wants to hang out with us! We can't be content with being just a slave. He wants to have discussions with us about the things that we love, the problems that keep us awake at night, the issues in life that make us question the goodness of humanity, or the plans for our future. All the conversations we might have with a human friend can be had with Jesus, and the great thing is that, not only does he want to talk with you, his advice is also so much better than what any other friend could offer.

 A few months ago I shared with a group of friends that one of my goals is to have a cup of coffee with Jesus. I get up pretty early most mornings to pray, and there is almost always a coffee cup in my hand, or close by, during these times. Sometimes I sit on the couch sipping coffee as I chat with the Lord, and I would really love it if he would physically show up, and enjoy a cup of dark roasted Columbian with me. I wonder if he's a black coffee kind of guy, or if he prefers a little cream, and sugar. It would be a pretty amazing opportunity, and I can't help, but take a quick look around the living room each morning to see if I have a guest. I know, that sounds a little crazy. Part of me used to think that this was an odd thing to want until I heard another speaker mention that he has the same desire. But he actually takes this a bit further by literally pouring a cup of coffee each morning for Jesus. Realistically I suppose it's not that strange because who wouldn't want to have a cup of coffee with Jesus? Who wouldn't jump at an opportunity to have that type of conversation? I doubt even an atheist would refuse the opportunity to sit with someone who he didn't think existed. And since I'm his friend, and he is always welcome in my life, then he is also always invited to join me. It hasn't happened yet. Maybe he's just waiting for me to get some better coffee. But if it ever does happen, I have a whole list of questions ready to go. Though I suspect those questions will quickly get tossed aside in favor of hearing what he has to say. The point is this, being a friend gives us access that others don't have.

You have the authority to speak for Jesus[8]

When kings hire ambassadors they delegate to them the authority to speak on behalf of the king. Ambassadors learn what the king wants, what he likes, and dislikes, his strategies, and his goals for expanding the kingdom. They study all the nuances of the king's plan for his kingdom because when they interact with others they must do so as a representative of the king. Ambassadors don't speak their own opinions; they only speak the opinions of the one who sent them. They interact with others in this way because their position also enables them to speak with the authority of the king. This is true for presidents, prime ministers, or any other leader who needs to send someone out as a representative. When you act as someone's representative you have to represent them the same way they would represent themselves. All Christians have the authority to speak on Jesus' behalf. Think about what happens when Jesus speaks; worlds are created, universes spring into being, life is formed when words fly from his lips. That sets the bar pretty high for someone who represents Jesus. And it also shows the level of authority we carry in the earth. Your words are incredibly powerful. Proverbs[9] tells us that the tongue has the power of life, and death. As Jesus' representative you get the opportunity to speak his life into people's lives. You don't represent yourself, you represent him. You don't speak your words, you speak his words. Jesus even said you can speak to a mountain, and cause it to be tossed into the sea[10]. So when you interact with other people you have the authority to speak into their lives the very things they need. I often declare peace over those struggling with fear, or anxiety, and joy over those suffering from depression. And when I pray for the sick I command the parts of the body to be well because that's how Jesus would do it. I speak from the perspective of the king I represent because I know what his will is.

Knowing who you are, knowing your true identity, is the key to effectively representing Jesus on earth. Too many Christians live from a skewed perspective of identity, and then end up living a life of lack. I think it is actually part of the enemy's strategy to keep us from knowing who we really are. As long as he can keep us in the dark he doesn't have to worry about a threat to his kingdom. But once we figure it out, the tables get turned, and his hold on this world slips away a little bit more. That rattles him, and he has to go on the offensive to scare us back into the hiding place of a false identity. But when you know who you are these little attacks become meaningless. All it takes is a look at a couple of scriptures to remind us that our purpose, and our role on this earth is so much more than most of us are living up to. As you read this you might be thinking to yourself that it doesn't apply to you. That God only uses a select few people in powerful ways, and that this identity applies to them, but everyone else is simply normal. I guarantee you this isn't true. When you accept Christ, your identity gets tied to his. When you accept Christ all of the attributes he has spoken over you become a reality. In 2 Corinthians[11] we are told that when we accept Christ we are transformed into a new creation. That applies to everyone who accepts Christ, and he wants everyone to step into that reality, and start flavoring the earth with his love.

When you know your identity your faith takes off to a whole new level. I didn't fully understand my identity when I first starting praying for sick people. I understood some of it, but it hadn't really sunk into my spirit yet. I would come home a little discouraged after not seeing any miracles, and of course, the enemy would take a few shots at me to make me feel worse. But I kept pressing on, and kept praying for people, mostly out of a tenacious hope that eventually I would get a breakthrough. God likes to teach us through our experiences, and I certainly learned a lot as I kept going for it, and kept failing. Some failures build character, but more importantly, it drove me back to God each time I didn't see a miracle take place. I'd go back to him, and ask for more of his presence, and greater breakthroughs because I had to see people healed. The truth is, I still do the same thing today. I'll see 25 people healed in one location, and only one healed somewhere else a few hours later, and that drives me back to his presence asking for more. At some point the tenacity I started with turned into a refusal to accept anything less than a miracle. This was the turning point for me as it was the point I began to realize my identity. And then I saw three miracles in just a matter of a few minutes. Not long after that I saw a few more people get healed. It started happening a couple times each month then grew to once a week, and now the miracles occur every time I have an opportunity to pray for someone. Sometimes it's a physical miracle, other times it's an emotional healing, and sometimes it's the incredible miracle of the love of God impacting someone's situation. All of this flows from intimacy with the Father within the perfect relationship as his son, or daughter.

When you know who you are, you start to look at the world differently. The same people that you used to avoid now become the ones you look for. I actively look for opportunities to release God's kingdom everywhere I go because I know who I am, and I know the authority that I carry can bring a change to any situation. One of my most common prayers is for God to let me see people through his eyes, and to give me his compassion. I don't ever want to walk past a person in need, and not give them what God has placed in my hands. That's where identity will take you. Because of your identity you have the ability to declare miracles into people's lives. And the great thing is that God wants to do miracles through you. In John 15[12] Jesus talked about how bearing much fruit brought glory to the Father. When he does a miracle through you it brings the Father glory. So it's not just you wanting to see a miracle, the Father wants to use you to do the miracle.

We all pick up different identities in life. Some people call me

Doctor. In other circles I am known as Reverend. And I picked up a few more titles while in the military. But none of those titles matter. I could throw them all in the trash today, and it wouldn't affect me because the only title I really care about, the only identity I really care about, is what God has given to me.

Endnotes
1. Matthew 10:8
2. Luke 10:1, 9
3. Matthew 5:14
4. Matthew 5:13
5. Ephesians 2:6
6. Romans 8:17
7. John 15:15
8. Mark 13:34
9. Proverbs 18:21
10. Mark 11:23
11. 2 Corinthians 5:17
12. John 15:8

Going Deeper

1. Is there anything in this chapter that made you re-think your true identity?

---

2. Do you really believe what God says about you?

---

3. How do your beliefs need to shift so that you can fully embrace the identity God has for you?

---

4. Are there any specific lies you have believed about your God given identity? Are you willing to get rid of them?

Deeper Declaration

I want to end this chapter with an identity statement that Rodney Hogue perfectly weaved together from a handful of different scriptures. This is a great tool for Christians to recite as a reminder of who they are. This is powerful for a couple of reasons. First, because it is the word of God, and second, because when your words come into agreement with his words it impacts your environment in amazing ways. I keep a copy of this in my bible as a constant reminder, and recite it over myself on a regular basis. Read through this, recite it out loud, and get it into your spirit.

"I am a child of the King. I am a co-heir with Jesus. All Jesus bought, and paid for is my inheritance. I am united with Jesus. I have been crucified with Christ. I died with Him, I was buried with Him, and I was raised with Him. I am seated with Him in the heavenlies far above all rule, all power, all authority, every dominion, and above every name that is named, not only in this age, but also in the one to come. Therefore I carry the authority of Christ. I have authority over sickness, over sin, over the flesh, over demons, and over the world. I am the salt of the earth; I am the light of the world. I will displace the darkness. I have the full armor of God. I put on the breastplate of righteousness, the belt of truth, the helmet of salvation, the sandals of peace, I take up the shield of faith, and the sword of the Spirit, for the weapons of my warfare are not fleshly. They are divinely powerful to tear down the strongholds of darkness. I can do all things through Christ, because greater is He who is in me than he who is in the world."

CHAPTER THREE

FULLY PAID

To most people in the city it was a typical Passover weekend. There were no special events scheduled for their busy lives. The majority of the population moved throughout the city with no real regard for what was happening on the other side of town. Employees went to work as usual, the various markets, and street vendors were open for business, and the town pace was as steady as any other day. But a crowd was forming on the far side of town. A man was arrested in the middle of the night, and was now being brought before the occupying Roman army to determine his fate. The charges were not enough to warrant any real punishment, but the crowd, which was quickly turning into an angry mob, demanded that this man be punished with death. And so the day's events quickly turned directions, and this man who just a week earlier rode into town to the tune of the peoples praise was now facing death for a simple crime against the local religious, organization; a crime which he did not commit, but the charges were trumped up because he posed a threat to the religious system that greatly influenced, and sometimes controlled the Jewish population. Although the punishment of death would be severe, this man knew that the very reason he was born was to lay down his life as a sacrifice, so no other human would ever have to suffer true death.

And he willingly accepted this punishment under the pretense that the reason for his death was for a far more noble cause than anyone in the crowd could fathom.

A lot was accomplished in the moment that Jesus died on the cross. The chasm that Adam, and Eve opened when they disobeyed in the garden was suddenly closed. The authority Satan had been given was taken back, and humanities, original relational connection to God was restored. We could once again walk with God in the cool of the day. We could have a real relationship with the one who first created, and breathed life into humanity. The record books full of the debt that we owed were thrown away. The debt for sin was fully paid for, and never again would anyone need to sacrifice, or be sacrificed for the purpose of forgiveness. The veil that separated man from God was torn away, and we could now freely access our creator without the need for a human mediator. Salvation had come. The powers of darkness were disarmed once, and for all. The enemy was shamefully defeated, and everything he had constructed came crashing down around him. Authority over the earth was returned to man. Authority over the enemy was also given to man. True peace was now available for everyone who pursued it. In fact, everything God had stored in his kingdom became available for anyone who believed enough to reach up, and take hold of it. The street was paved for the arrival of the Holy Spirit, and for the gifts that he would give. None of those gifts were limited to just a few people, nor were they limited to a specific time period. They were made available for all people, and all time. This is the, original epic story. The world would never be the same again. The cross brought more than salvation, it also brought deliverance for the oppressed, and healing for the sick. All of it was fully paid for at the same time.

Salvation is the central message of most churches because it's the most important element of what Jesus provided for us when he died. Without his sacrifice we could never be right with God. It is the death of Jesus that paid for the forgiveness of all our sins. Without the salvation that Jesus provided through his sacrifice, we would be forced to sacrifice animals on a regular basis just to push the punishment for sins a little further down the road. Hebrews 10[1] says that is impossible for the blood of bulls, and goats to take away sins. The blood of a sacrificed animal never saved anyone! I don't know about you, but I'm sure glad I don't have to deal with cutting open an animal, and burning it on an altar every year. I don't even hunt, or fish because I don't want anything to do with gutting, and cleaning an animal after the kill. Thank God for supermarkets! But it's more than just saving us from the squeamishness of dealing with animal guts. The Old Testament system of sacrifice was never designed, or intended to last forever. It was a shadow pointing the coming of the Messiah who would offer a perfect sacrifice on our behalf. It provided a temporary stay of execution, but not forgiveness. The prophet Hosea[2] told us that what God really desires is mercy, not sacrifice, and the acknowledgment of God rather than burnt offerings. God's mercy was shown in the death on the cross because it brought about complete forgiveness from every aspect, and consequence of sin. Year after year the people would bring their offerings for a sacrifice, and each time they were reminded of the sins they had committed. There was no freedom from guilt. They still carried the shame, and the pain of what they had done wrong. We don't have to carry guilt anymore.

Your sins are completely forgiven. There is no need for you to worry about your past mistakes, or think that somehow God is punishing you for sins that he already forgave. When you accepted Jesus you become a new creation; 2 Corinthians[3] declares that we are a new creation. So many Christians live a life of despair thinking that their past has disqualified them from being anything more than what they already are. That is so untrue. They think that they could never be used by God, and relegate themselves to their perception of what an average Christian life should look like. Salvation doesn't just get you into heaven, it gives you access to everything in heaven. Salvation doesn't just wipe away your sins it sets you free from them! Your sins are in the past, and they need to stay there. God tosses out the record book filled with all the lies, deceit, and maliciousness we were involved in before we came to the cross. When asked for forgiveness, he simply forgives, forgets, and moves on. Some say it's only ok to look at your past through the blood of Jesus; that's a fair analysis, but I think we can take it a step further by not even looking at it. God doesn't remember your sins anymore, so there's no reason for you to dwell on that period of your life either. When you are reminded of your past, take a moment, and thank God for his mercy, and his grace. The enemy hates it when God receives glory, so whenever he pops up to remind me about anything I am quick to turn it around, and give glory to God. Do that often enough, and he will stop reminding you. Your past doesn't disqualify you from anything!

You don't have to wait until you are perfect to serve. You can start right now. I saw a bumper sticker once that said "Christians aren't perfect, their just forgiven." It seems like a cop out to shirk responsibility, but it's true. We are not made perfect in an instant. It takes time to get from the point of realizing what Jesus did for us to the point of being perfected by his grace. I seriously doubt any person on the planet other than Jesus ever walked in the status of perfection. So we can't take the approach that we will start serving God after we get everything straightened out in our lives. No one would ever serve if that was the case. We see in Philippians[4] that "he who began a good work in you will carry it on to completion until the day of Christ Jesus." The work has been started, but it may not have been completed yet. So we cannot use the "I'm just not good enough" excuse anymore. We all need to have a few rough edges removed, and a few wrinkles to be ironed out. But as we spend time in his presence, and work on his behalf the glory that he shines on us brings about the changes we need. Again in 2 Corinthians[5] we see that we are "being transformed into his image with ever-increasing glory." Other translations say "from glory to glory." I like that. God carries us from glory to glory until the work he has started is completed. There's no reason to sit on the pew, and do nothing. Salvation gives all of us the ability to step out, and represent Jesus even as we continue to learn how to represent him. But there is more.

Every sickness, and every disease must bow at the feet of Jesus.

Isaiah 53[6] tells us another part of the story. It says that "by his wounds we are healed." It's a phrase that often plays second fiddle to salvation, but is equally important because without it we would be destined to live a life full of pain, and suffering. This verse shows us that the blood that was spilled on the ground that day was also so that we can be healed. Every sickness, and every disease must bow at the feet of Jesus. There is no healing he didn't pay for. There is no disease he didn't defeat on that day. If you have enough faith to believe in salvation, you also have enough faith to believe for healing. It's the same amount of faith because it was paid for through the same event. You don't have to think that you don't have enough faith for healing. If you are a follower of Jesus, you already have enough faith to see miracles happen. Healing was a pivotal part of Jesus' ministry. He healed the sick everywhere he went, and instructed the disciples to do the same. God had purposed for this to continue, and throughout the New Testament we see evidence of this as he healed time, and time again through the apostles, through Paul, and through others.

When we believe in salvation without believing in healing, we limit the work Jesus did at the cross. Somewhere during the timespan between the ministry of the apostles, and today many Christians came up with the notion that healing was no longer for today. They think the miraculous was only available during the lives of the apostles to help lay the foundation of the church, or validate their ministry, but that it all ended with their deaths. This cessasionist idea is a lie, and it has robbed the church of so many blessings while at the same time denying the work of the Holy Spirit. In the past century alone we have seen a renewal of the Holy Spirit being poured out on the earth, and thousands are healed every week through just a handful of ministries. There are churches, and itinerate ministers partnering with God today that many of you reading this book have never heard of. The funny thing is that they are the ones doing the real work of the church. They are the ones bringing healing to the sick on city streets, seeing amazing miracles in South American revivals, and converting millions of Muslims to Christianity in the Middle East. The question every believer who doesn't see miracles happening all around them should be asking is, "why don't I see miracles in my church?" There are some who believe in healing, but don't actively pursue it, so they never see anything supernatural happen. Someone needing prayer will be added to a prayer list instead of anyone actively engaging a little faith, and praying for them on the spot. And when people are actually prayed for in a church no one ever dares to ask if the person feels better because there is no expectation of anything ever happening. Prayer lists aren't bad, but they are very passive. Jesus wasn't passive in anything he did, if anything he was aggressive. He aggressively pursued sickness by healing people every day.

The more your faith grows the more risk you will take.

It's already done. It's already accomplished. You don't have to fight for it, Jesus already paid for it. You just have to take hold of it by faith. The same amount of faith needed to believe in Christ is the same amount needed to receive a healing. The same amount of faith needed to see a toenail grow back is the same amount needed to see a cancerous tumor disappear. Jesus said it only takes the faith of a mustard seed to move a mountain[7]. The thing that's great about that example is that a mustard seed grows up into a huge tree. Your faith also grows as you step out with the authority God has already given you, and start to pray with an expectation that miraculous things will happen just the way Jesus said they would. It might start out small like a tiny mustard seed, but just like a muscle that grows with regular exercise, your faith will also grow. And the more your faith grows the more risk you will take. We often associate different types of sickness with more risk. We think that praying for someone with a headache is easier than praying for someone who is missing a finger. I guess that's just human nature, but it's a little funny because we are not the ones doing the healing; God is the healer, and nothing is difficult for him. So whether you are praying for someone with a common cold, or for someone in a wheelchair who has never walked before, neither is hard for God, and one is certainly not harder than the other. But when I think of taking greater risk I'm talking about being sensitive to the voice of Holy Spirit, and being willing to pray for anyone you encounter, no matter where you are, whenever he directs you to do so. This could be in supermarkets, on sidewalks, or anywhere else your daily life may take you.

It can create a scene, especially when God shows up, and heals them. It's impossible to not be impacted when God heals you, and even the random onlookers will be amazed at what just happened. Praying for people inside the walls of a church is easy. Taking it outside the church walls is the hard part. In fact I think the reason why Jesus sent the disciple in groups of two was for peer pressure. It's a lot easier to pray for a stranger when the guy next to you is jabbing you in the ribs, and telling you to go for it. We prayed for a young man's legs in a parking lot one day that created quite a scene. He had broken both of his legs a year earlier, and they still hadn't completely healed. After a short prayer, I told him to test them out, so he started to run through the parking lot. He ran back, and forth to a building about 100 feet away. Then he started running in circles through the parking lot while approximately 30 people stood around wondering what was happening. One person yelled out, "do you get the Holy Ghost?" It was exciting, and funny all at the same time. And it had a lasting impact, not just in this young man's life, but also in the lives of everyone else who witnessed a miracle.

Let me add one more thought before I move on. Everything is easy for God, but that doesn't make any of it less important. God deserves our praise every day, and when he actively involves himself by providing a miracle it's even more reason for us to celebrate his goodness. So I'll repeat the earlier example, it doesn't matter if it's a common cold, or someone in a wheelchair who has never walked before. If God fixes the problem, it is a miracle, and it should be celebrated. Everything God does is miraculous. It's in his nature. It's who he is. But there is still more.

Supernatural healing is not always physical. There is a spiritual element to healing as well because sometimes the wounds that we carry cannot be seen by the natural eye. Everyone encounters different hardships in life, and those hardships can leave their mark in the form of personal emotions like depression, addiction, loneliness, fear, or anger. That's a short list, but you get the point. Life can leave us scarred in ways others can't always ,see, or detect. I think this is best described as a soul wound. When we sin, or when others sin against us it can create a wound on our souls that doesn't necessarily get healed at the point of salvation. These wounds stand out in the spiritual realm, and give the enemy a target to attack. People notice when we are physically wounded because they can see the injury. I don't know what it looks like exactly in the spirit realm, but the wound is somehow visible to the spirits that occupy that realm. When you have a wounded soul, the enemy can look at it, and attack according to the wound you carry. And if the attack is successful they can even make the wound bigger, and begin to establish footing in your life. For example, let's say you grew up in a home full of anger where your parents were always fighting with each other, and yelling at you. That type of environment can leave you with a lot of issues as you grow older, and you will most likely end up being an angry person as well. When the enemy sees that anger wound he comes alongside you, and tries to influence your thoughts in a way to respond angrily in situations. If this goes on long enough that spirit will end up having a level of control over you that keeps you angry all the time. The same is true for a lot of other emotions, and while it would be foolish to think that every emotional problem is demonically influenced, I do think that people with severe cases of things like bad self-esteem, anger, and depression probably have a spirit hanging over them, and the worst part, is that they don't even know it's happening.

Christians aren't exempt from demonic activity either. I was told all my life that Christians couldn't be possessed, and I still believe that to be true, but I have learned that there are other ways the enemy can influence us without taking complete control of our lives. Those wounds I mentioned earlier are a good starting point. I've heard some refer to them as "cling-ons" because they cling onto us, and don't let go unless someone tells them to leave. They cling onto those wounds either before, or after you accept Christ, and just stick around. They don't always have the authority to be there, but they will stick around until someone tells them to leave. If you are struggling with an issue that you just can't seem to get rid of on your own then you should ask the Holy Spirit to reveal to you if your problems are spiritually influenced. Your soul is made up of your mind, will, and emotions, and it's easy for the enemy to hide his influence in those areas of your life. It doesn't need to be dramatic after you discover what's going on, just command them to leave, and watch how quickly you feel differently.

Deliverance is a subject rarely tackled by pastors in their morning sermons, or even in their weekly staff meetings. People don't like to talk about demons because it scares them. They probably won't admit to that fact, but it's true. We tend to be afraid of what we don't know, and when it comes to the subject of the demonic there is a lot we don't know. There are plenty of great books on deliverance that cover this subject in depth, but the point I want to get across here is that Jesus' death provided you, a disciple of Jesus, with authority over the demonic forces that try to influence you, and others every day. Pastors are essentially taking a stance of avoidance when they don't teach the body the importance of this authority, or how to use it. If anyone thinks that demons are just sitting a room somewhere twiddling their thumbs with nothing to do, they are hugely mistaken. Demons are actively working to mess up what God is doing. They are actively pursuing human targets to create disruption, and I tend to think that they are only successful when we are not doing our job. Demons come into my house every now, and then, and when they do I just tell them to leave. The angels can stay as long as they like, but the demons are not welcome. I used to be afraid of evil spiritual activity, but when I learned about the authority I had that fear was replaced with annoyance, and now I'm indifferent because I know they have no influence over me. There's no reason to be afraid.

God has already given you authority over the demonic forces. We already talked about identity, so now I want to link your identity to your authority. Your identity gives you authority over a wide range of areas to include the realm of demonic forces. When you come in contact with people who are oppressed by these spirits you have the authority to send them on their way. When Jesus sent out the 72 disciples they returned with a pretty amazing statement. They said even the demons were submitting to them in Jesus' name[8]. But it wasn't just a simple factual statement of what had occurred; they were excited that they could dispatch the enemy simply from the perspective of the authority Jesus had given to them when he sent them out. When you have authority you don't have to fight for control. The demons at the tomb in Mark 5[9] didn't fight with Jesus; it was actually quite the opposite. They freaked out as soon as he walked up, and immediately started to beg for permission to stay. They recognized authority, and didn't even consider fighting. Later in Acts[10] we see a story about the Seven sons of Sceva who were trying to cast out demons without having any authority because they weren't believers in Christ. The demons actually taunted them about not knowing who they were, and the possessed man overpowered, and beat them to the point that they ran away naked, and bleeding. The demons recognize authority, and they recognize a lack of authority. A more current example of delegated authority can be found in the power a police officer carries through the badge they wear on their chest. They have been granted authority to enforce laws, and maintain peace, and there is no question who is in charge when they arrive at a crime scene. Most civilians will follow the direction of police officers without any resistance, but if another person with no authority began to give direction they would receive a different response. Authority gives the police the power to keep the peace, and our authority gives us the same right in the spiritual realm.

That's a lot of information to digest, so let me sum it all up with this. Salvation heals your spirit, deliverance heals your soul, and physical healing heals your body. It was all fully paid for on the cross, so reach out, and take hold of it. Don't limit yourself to just part of what Jesus paid for; being a Christian isn't limited to just getting to heaven. There is so much more he accomplished for us that enables us to live a life of power, authority, and influence in the world. You should be using the authority he has given you to make the world around you a better place.

Endnotes
1. Hebrews 10:4
2. Hosea 6:6
3. 2 Corinthians 5:17
4. Philippians 1:6
5. 2 Corinthians 3:18
6. Isaiah 53:5
7. Matthew 17:20
8. Luke 10:17
9. Mark 5:1-14
10. Acts 19:13-16

Going Deeper

1. Is there anything you don't believe Jesus paid for at the cross?

---

2. Have you had any life experiences that have kept you from believing in God's desire, or ability to perform miracles?

---

3. Are you willing to live a risk taking life that brings physical, emotional, and spiritual healing to others?

---

4. What is one miracle you need right now?

Deeper Prayer

We all start with a measure of faith, and we all need to have our faith increased to believe for God to do even more in, and through our lives. If you desire more faith, I invite you to pray this prayer:

Jesus, just as I have believed that you paid for my salvation, I declare today that I also believe you paid for the supernatural healing of every sickness, and disease that can affect a person's body, or soul. I believe that you are the God of miracles. I believe what you said in John 15:7, that I will receive anything I ask for as long as I remain in relationship with you. I ask today for an increase in my faith. Increase my faith to believe for greater miracles than I have ever seen, or heard about. You said that we would perform greater miracles than you did, so I ask today for that to be evident in my life. Give me the boldness to step out in faith with an expectation that you will show up, and show off when I pray, no matter what the need is in front of me. Use me for your glory.

CHAPTER FOUR

PARTNERS

Imagine you were starting a new business, and the richest man in the world called you up one day to say that he wanted to be your partner. It's probably the dream of most entrepreneurs that a wealthy person would agree to partner with them on a business venture because it would be pretty difficult to fail if you had several hundred billion dollars backing your ideas. Suddenly, at that point, you would have all the resources you need to be successful. Advertising, development, and production would become an overnight reality. The financial resources from a partner like that would be incredible. And then you would also have access to established connections with other business leaders. Wealthy businessmen know other wealthy businessmen, and can connect you with other people who could help get your ideas, and products into the hands of consumers. World class contacts, suppliers, and clients would be at your fingertips, and your product would end up on store shelves in record time. Starting a business on your own with little money, or resources is difficult, and the odds of success are pretty low. It's hard to get traction on a new venture even if you have the greatest idea ever conceived by a human mind. That's where the value of having a great partner comes into play. Even as the junior partner with little to bring to the game, you are still guaranteed success when your partner provides all the resources, and the only risk that you carry is the reputation of being connected to that partner. Of course, the chances of scoring the world's wealthiest man as a business partner are pretty low. In fact, the odds are probably better at winning the lottery, but there is someone with even more resources who would love to partner with you.

Now, imagine that God called you up one day, and said he wanted to be your partner. Well, it would probably be more like he wanted you to partner with him. And once again all the resources you could ever need to be successful in this venture would be available to you. But this partnership would be more than just a little different because the resources God can provide truly are unlimited in every way. We don't have any power, but he has all the power. We can't heal anyone, but he can heal everyone. Miracles are his specialty, not ours. The great part about it is that God created us for the purpose of partnering with us. Plenty of books have been written about how to find your purpose, but it can be summed up very simply by saying this; your purpose is to partner with God. Think about that for a minute, and let it soak in. God wants to partner with you! The same one who spoke the world into existence wants to use your life to impact the world. Now, that does seem a little odd because God could very easily speak anything, and everything he wants into, or out of existence. He doesn't need a partner. He doesn't need any help from anyone, especially not from the people that he created. If anything, we create more work for him. But even though all that is true, he created us to partner with him. Most people enjoy collaborating with others on projects because it's more fun to share those experiences with others than to do it by ourselves. I doubt God was bored, but I do think he created us to play a part in his master plan, and it really isn't complete without each one of us playing our role.

Ok, so at this point you are probably wondering about what it means to partner with God. I've already shared a little bit about what it means to me, and I'll share some more as we go forward, but for now let's take a look at what it meant to a few people who you have probably already read about somewhere else. If you're reading this book, you have probably heard of the story about Daniel, and the lion's den. If you haven't, go take a quick read of Daniel chapter six, and then come back here. That story is pretty amazing by itself because it shows us that Daniel must have had an amazing relationship with God if he sent an angel to hold back a cave full of lions. He was tossed into a lion's den for breaking a stupid law that prohibited him from praying, but God didn't let the story end in that cave. It's hard for others not to notice when God does something miraculous in their midst. The Bible tells us how the Babylonian king reacted to this incident, but I have to wonder how the rest of the community reacted. Daniel must have been marked by the people as someone special. Later, we see stories about other angels visiting Daniel to have conversations with him on what seems like a regular basis. Of course, each chapter in his book doesn't equally correlate with several days in the same week, but I think just one encounter with an angel would be enough to mark someone as a partner with God. And when angels show up to reveal to you, in graphic detailed imagery, the future of the world, to include the final epic battle between God, and Satan, it elevates your reputation to a whole new level. We see that Daniel had something special. He was a partner with God.

Long before Daniel we find another man whose days prior to our introduction to him are shrouded in mystery. What we do know is that God saw something in him, and called him to be his partner. It took a lot of risk, but Abraham, or Abram as he was known then, packed up his home, and took a road trip to relocate to where God directed him. Our first glimpse into this relationship is found in Genesis 12[1] where God tells Abraham that he's going to bless him, and make him a great nation, but there is a cost attached. There is always a cost attached to partnering with God. Abraham had to leave most of his family behind as he journeyed to a new land to start a new life. And he spent the rest of his life hearing God audibly speak to him, entertaining angels who showed up at his campsite, and laying the foundation for what would eventually become God's chosen nation. There were a lot of adventures along the way as he encountered Egyptian Pharaohs[2], fought in battle against the kings of neighboring cities to rescue his relatives[3], and was even prepared to sacrifice his own son if that's what God required[4]. One man took a risk to partner with God, and a nation was born that has outlasted every other nation, and empire established since that time. Partnering with God brings about amazing results that we could never achieve on our own. Abraham could have ignored God, and stayed with his family, but then we probably would have never heard of him, and this paragraph would be about someone else. But Abraham accepted the challenge, took the risk of being obedient, even if it made him look foolish, and ultimately helped shape the history of the world.

The least in the Kingdom of Heaven is greater than John the Baptist.

You know what stands out to me the most about these guys? They lived before the crucifixion of Jesus. They lived before the infilling of the Holy Spirit was released to all mankind. Jesus said in Luke 7[5] that John the Baptist was the greatest of all the prophets, and then he went onto say that the least in the kingdom of heaven is greater than John the Baptist. These guys lived in an era where accessing the kingdom of heaven was not as easy as it is today. The sacrifice of Jesus changed the dynamic to how we approach God, and yet these other prophets of the Old Testament who lived hundreds of years earlier had audible conversations with God, and with angels, and saw amazing visions. I'll be the first to admit that it makes me a little jealous! If they were able to partner with God in that era, and have such great accomplishments that people are still talking about it thousands of years later, we certainly have an opportunity to impact the world in an even greater way today. God wanted to partner with them, and he wants to partner with you. I don't know if it's any easier to partner with God today than it was back then, but I do know that we have more available to us today. Jesus' sacrifice opened up the storehouses of heaven, and gave us access to everything within his kingdom. The patriarchs of old were limited in what they could access because Jesus had not yet come to sacrifice his life on their behalf. That sacrifice restored the relationship we have with God back to what Adam, and Eve had before they sinned. Then the gift of the Holy Spirit, and the gifts of the Holy Spirit, were added on top of that to empower us in new ways.

I had a dream once where I was walking down the hallway of the building we lived in, and as I came to our condominium, I saw a pile of salt on the ground in front of the door. When I woke up the next morning I pondered the meaning of this dream, and began to search the scriptures for references to salt, so I could properly interpret what God was showing me. Salt is only mentioned about 35 times in the Bible, so it didn't take long to read through those references. Most of them didn't have any application to this dream, but two of those verses stood out as particularly interesting. The first is in Numbers 18[6] where the phrase "covenant of salt" first appears in the Bible, and the second is in 2 Chronicles 13[7] where the same phrase appears again. This covenant of salt is only mentioned twice in the Bible, and now my soul was burning to know what it meant. As I dug deeper I learned about a Jewish custom where people would share salt to solidify, and preserve their friendship. This is when the Lord told me he was establishing an everlasting covenant of salt with me. My first thought was, wow! Then my second thought was, why me? I imagine similar thoughts went through the mind of Abraham when God called him, but there I was standing next to the sink in my bathroom when God revealed his desire to be my friend. To be fair I already knew of Jesus' discussion about friendship with his disciples in John 15[8], but this experience made the idea real to me. I believe it is God's desire to be friends with, and partner with every human on the planet, and to seal that friendship with a covenant of salt.

Adam, and Eve were the, original partners with God. He planted an amazing garden, and put them in charge of maintaining what he had created. He gave Adam the awesome responsibility of naming every member of the animal kingdom, and God literally walked with Adam in the garden on a regular basis. I imagine the conversations they had on those walks were nothing short of amazing. What do you talk about with the one who just created you a few days earlier? I'm sure there were discussions about how to care for the different trees, how to prune back the grape vines to produce a better crop, and how to retrieve fresh honey from a beehive without getting stung. God charged these, original pioneers with the job of filling, and subduing the earth. Essentially their role was to expand the territory of the garden until it covered the entire earth. They would need other hands to help with the maintenance, so having kids, and ultimately creating a community, was also part of the process. If all went well the world would have eventually been one giant garden with a whole lot of naked people; though the naked part would probably be a little weird. Everyone knows it didn't take long for the story to fall apart when the gardeners chose to take a different direction than what God had instructed. God gave them dominion, and authority over the earth, but when they foolishly accepted Satan's challenge that God had lied to them, they relinquished that dominion, and authority to another. This is why when Satan later tempted Jesus in Luke 4^9 he was able to offer up the authority over the earth in return for worship. Authority was given to man, man gave it to Satan, and Satan offered it to Jesus who refused the deal, and then later took it back by force, and offered it once again to man. The possibility of partnership was once again restored.

God is still looking for someone to partner with today. His eyes range throughout the earth to find someone who is committed to him, and when he finds that person, he puts the full weight of his strength behind his new partner[10]. When I read that verse in 2 Chronicles, I immediately start to wonder about what he is looking for. When God's eyes scan the surface of the earth, and look across all of humanity, what stands out to him as something worthy of strengthening? The verse gives us a clue with the phrase "fully committed." That leaves us with the task of deciphering what it means to be fully committed;, or maybe we don't. Maybe we just take the text at face value. The, original Hebrew word used here is also rendered in other versions, and verses as complete, perfect, just, and made ready. I like the connotation of fully committed because it seems to carry the idea of being connected to his purpose, and I think that's the key to partnering with God. There's a big difference between us partnering with what God wants, and God partnering with what we want. When we link into what he is doing we are guaranteed success. In Matthew 5^{11} Jesus said, "the Son can do nothing by himself; he can do only what he sees his Father doing, because whatever the Father does the Son also does." He didn't say "the Father only does what he sees the Son doing." I think we could rephrase that by saying, we partner with God, God doesn't partner with us. On the surface that sounds like God doesn't care about what we want, but that's not what I mean. Jesus said in Matthew 6^{12} to "seek first his kingdom, and his righteousness." You can't be so heavenly minded that you are no earthly good, so there must be some middle ground there, right?

He wants your focus on him first.

Here's the reality, God is not sitting in heaven saying "hey just sit next to me, and don't worry about earth. Earth will take care of itself." God cares about everything happening on the planet! He cares about your needs, and your desires. But he tells us to seek him first because he already knows what we need, and is fully capable of providing for all of that. He wants your focus on him first, but he doesn't want you to just hang out with him all the time. He's not looking for someone to play dominoes with. He wants you to be intimately involved in the details of his plan for creation, and actively engaged in that mission.

Really, I think that when you are fully partnering with him you are also fully in his presence at the same time. So when you tell God that you want to do whatever he wants you to, he gets excited. I can almost picture him jumping up off of the throne, and screaming "Yes! I've been waiting for you to say that!" And then, he starts lining up your assignments. For some it might be digging wells in Africa, so the people can have clean fresh water. For others it might be freeing victims of human trafficking, and bringing their slave owners to justice. Some might even be used in corporate settings to fulfill God's purposes in medical, science, education, and other fields. Regardless of the mission, there is always a guarantee that everything you do for him will have the purpose of bringing his kingdom to earth, and nothing bad can ever come from the expansion of his kingdom. So we partner with him, and then he takes care of all the peripheral needs that pop up along the way.

When the world we live in encounters his kingdom everything in our reality changes to match his reality.

Ok, so how do we partner with God? The simple answer is to do what Jesus did. Jesus gave us the perfect example of partnership because everything he did was to please the Father. If you read through the gospels you'll find that Jesus kept talking about the kingdom of heaven. Everywhere he went, he was describing this kingdom, and telling people it had come near to them. His life was about his kingdom because when the world we live in encounters his kingdom, everything in our reality changes to match his reality. Everything he did was from a perspective of love, compassion, and mercy. Even in the harshness he showed to the Jewish leaders by routinely challenging their attitudes, and rebuffing their questions, we see a loving desire to bring correction, so that they too could be restored. If the religious leaders would have responded with a desire to follow Jesus, I'm confident he would have been happy to bring them into the fold. Sickness doesn't exist in his kingdom, so he healed sick people everywhere he went. Even in his home town where people only remembered him as the carpenter's son, he still brought part of his kingdom to them[13]. Romans 14[14] tells us that the kingdom of God is "righteousness, peace, and joy." That was the centrality of Jesus' message; preaching righteousness with a dose of joy, and peace.

I mentioned earlier that Jesus only did what he saw the father doing. I'll give you one example of what I do when I'm praying for someone who needs a miracle. I typically pray a short simple prayer that only lasts a few seconds, and then I ask the person if anything has changed, or if they are feeling any different. Usually one, or two short prayers are all it takes to get someone healed, so this is one way I test to see what God is doing. If there is any improvement at all with the symptoms, I know that God is doing something. If they are not completely healed, I pray another short prayer, and then have them test out their bodies one more time. I continue this process as long as there is improvement, or until the healing is complete. In these instances I see that the Father is healing, so I work alongside him by continuing to pray. For those who don't improve, or don't feel anything, I still continue to pray for them in the same manner as anyone else. I can't just give up, and walk away after a few seconds. I keep praying, and if after a few minutes nothing is happening, I encourage them that God wants to heal their bodies, and that they should continue seeking for a miracle. It's a delicate balance because I want to see everyone healed, but it's also about doing what the Father is doing, so I try not to spend a long time contending for a healing if I don't see any improvement. In both instances, I am partnering with God. One person is healed, and another is not. But even the unhealed person was blessed, and received a measure of God's love that they would not have received otherwise. I don't know why some remain unhealed, but as long as they feel loved, I have done my job.

Helping people in need is a good habit to have even if it is not from a Christian perspective. It's relatively easy to hand out sandwiches to the homeless, or donate clothing to a shelter, and both of these actions go a long way to show someone you care. But what if you could give them so much more than just a small meal, or a new pair of shoes? What if you had the ability to replace the fear in their lives with perfect peace? What if you could get them a brand new ankle to replace the one that's been injured for a long time? What if you were the conduit by which all the cancer in their body was destroyed? Do you think that would have a more lasting impact? I used to be able to put five dollars into a homeless guys hand, and feel like I made some major impact on his life. The truth is, I don't know what he used the money for, or even if he was homeless. But I figured doing something was better than nothing. I can't do that anymore, because it's not enough. I have so much more to give, and it's not enough to hand out spare change, and keep walking. I'm the light of the world, and I don't have the right to switch that light off. I'm the salt of the earth, and I don't have the right to keep the salt in my pocket. I have to spread the salt, and shine the light everywhere I go. So now when someone asks me for spare change, I usually offer to buy them a coffee, talk to them for a few minutes, and then sneak in a prayer; they always end up getting a lot more than they ever expected. Sometimes it's accompanied by a healing, but it's always a blessing because it's always accompanied by love.

If you've been paying attention you noticed I used the word partner a lot in this chapter. If you go back, and count you'll find I used it more than 40 times. Christian literally means follower of Christ, but I think in some ways it could be re-coined as "God's partner." The church has fallen into the trap of going to a building once, or twice a week to sing a few songs, and hear a good message, but it's a rarity to see the church go out into the communities to bring the kingdom of heaven as Jesus did. Some churches are certainly involved in partnering with God in this way, but those are few, and far between. People wonder why we have so many problems on the planet. They wonder why if God is love there could be so much needless violence. The answer is simple. The world is messed up because the Church isn't doing its job. If one church in every city would begin to partner with God by doing what Jesus did instead of just talking a good game on Sunday morning, the impact would be hugely measurable. Peace, and joy always follow in our wake when we go out on the streets to minister healing. When the kingdom of heaven invades a street corner there is a shift in the spiritual atmosphere that ripples through the entire spectrum of existence in that area. But the only way we can have lasting impact is if we continue to partner with God on a regular basis. Adam, and Eve were told to subdue the earth; that's a militaristic way of saying subject the earth to your control. When we operate from a kingdom perspective, the reality of that kingdom overtakes the reality of the physical world, and cancer disappears, bones regrow, hope is restored, lives are renewed, and the world is changed. Partnering with God has a greater impact than anything else we can ever do.

Endnotes
1. Genesis 12:1-9
2. Genesis 12:16
3. Genesis 14:14-16
4. Genesis 22:1-12
5. Luke 7:28
6. Numbers 18:19
7. 2 Chronicles 13:5
8. John 15:15
9. Luke 4:6-7
10. 2 Chronicles 16:9
11. Matthew 5:19
12. Matthew 6:33
13. Mark 6:5
14. Romans 14:17

Going Deeper

1. What is one thing you want to start partnering with God on?

---

2. Do you have any fear, or hesitation about partnering with him?

---

3. Do you want to see the kingdom of heaven manifested on the earth?

---

4. Ask God to show you one step you can take today to start partnering with him more. What did he say to you?

Deeper Prayer

Partnering with God is a lot of fun. It just takes a step of faith to get started. God wants to be your partner, and he wants to empower you to make a radical change on the earth. Pray this prayer, and watch as God brings the answer others need through your life:

Father, I want to see your kingdom come, not just as a model prayer, but in actual reality. I want to see the greatness of your kingdom impact the earth, and I want to partner with you in making it happen. Give me eyes to see what you are doing, and ears to hear what you are speaking, so that I can fully partner with you regardless of where I am. I renounce the lies of fear that have held me back, and I ask you today for greater measures of boldness to share your love with everyone I meet. I'm ready to take the next step, lead me, and I will follow you no matter where you take me.

CHAPTER FIVE

ACT LIKE A KID

Several years ago we traveled to Auckland, New Zealand as members of a Global Awakening team to minister at a church's healing conference. I had never been to New Zealand, and it was a great first visit that I will never forget. I learned a lot on that trip, but nothing more profound than what I observed on one of the first few days. I met Nick, this great Australian guy who had such a genuine desire to see God powerfully touch people that he didn't care what other people thought. Have you ever noticed how little kids really don't care what the people around them think? They'll run around playgrounds pretending to be all sorts of fictional characters as they play, and not even have a second thought about whether, or not someone might laugh at their silliness. Standing 6'7" tall no one would ever confuse Nick with a kid; that is until he starts to minister, and then you get a glimpse of Jesus' idea of childlike faith. Jesus once said in Matthew 18[1] that we need to become like little children if we want to enter into the kingdom of heaven. That could have been a reference to a childlike faith that believes in the existence of God, and that follows after Jesus with reckless abandon. But I think it has a deeper meaning. I think that there should be a childlike attitude in every part of our Christian walk.

What Nick taught me, not through his words, but through his

actions, was that we can act like kids, and have fun in church while we minister to others. If you've never seen someone fall down under the power of God, you probably won't understand this next part, so I should probably offer a small explanation. Sometimes, God's presence is so powerful that it literally knocks you over. One analogy to describe this would be standing in the ocean waiting for the waves to crash against your body. The smaller waves could probably knock you over if you aren't paying attention, and the larger waves will almost always take you down. If you have good footing you can usually keep yourself upright with the smaller waves, but the big waves will almost certainly knock you over. The presence of God tends to flow like ocean waves, and if you watch people closely when they are being prayed for in environments where there is a strong presence of God, sometimes you will see them shift one of their feet a little further back to keep from falling down. This is a tell-tale sign that they are being hit by one of those waves, and they don't want to fall down. But sometimes those waves are so strong that you don't even have time to shift your feet, and resist God's touch. Sometimes they come so quickly that you end up on the floor. That's one example of how our physical bodies react to the presence of his supernatural power. At other times, it has a completely different effect. As God's presence saturates a person they might start to look a little drunk. It's actually quite funny to watch people get drunk on God's presence because it is typically accompanied by a lot of laughter. I love watching God interact with his creation in this way, and I love releasing his joy into people's lives; it has become one of my favorite things to do.

Nick's idea of a good time was to go find people who looked like they were hungry for more of God, and then release some of those waves over them with the purposeful intention of leaving them drunk on the floor soaking in God's presence. He referred to it as whacking, which I think was his playful way of describing what was about to happen. If you've watched a few mob movies you know that mobsters, at least TV mobsters, use whacking as a phrase to kill people, but this has a different connotation. Actually, he had another phrase he used that I like even better; "whack 'em, and stack 'em." There were two things that struck me about these whacking sessions. First, the mere idea of looking for people to whack was pretty comical, and maybe even a little childlike. It reminded me a little of the freeze tag game we used to play as kids. Except instead of running around to give freedom from an imaginary frozen state we were giving freedom to enjoy God. The second thing that stood out to me was the way he prayed for people. He didn't use very many words, or go into a long flowing prayer. He simply touched them with his finger, and made a silly noise like bzzt, boom, or whoosh. I laughed when I heard him doing this, and I laughed even harder when the people started falling down. Sounds childlike right? On the surface it seems a little odd that God would cause his presence to flow through someone who essentially just looks like they are goofing off, but that's a humanistic way of thinking, and I'm glad God thinks, and operates differently, because prayer starts to look a little different when you know your true identity.

> **When you're his kid the conversation takes on a different tone.**

Most religious people take a very stoic serious approach to prayer. They view prayer as a sacramental conversation with God that should be approached in a serious manner. They aren't necessarily wrong. Having a conversation with the creator of the universe is important business, but when you're his kid the conversation takes on a different tone. I've been in churches where prayers were recited from a book instead of from the heart. I've heard people pray long prayers that were ineffective, and had little to no effect on the situation at hand. That's not to say that God didn't hear their prayers, but people in these situations are praying from the perspective of a servant instead of a child. We aren't strangers with the one we pray to, and we aren't casual acquaintances either. Even if you are a Christian that only opens the

Bible a few times a year, and barely prays every week, you are still his kid. Kids approach their parents from a childlike perspective, and with a childlike attitude of expectation. They never stop to think about what daddy can't do. They only assume he can do anything because their minds haven't been filled with other notions. They view every conversation with their parents as exciting, and fun. You can go to God with expectation, and you can have fun when you pray! You can act like a kid, and it's ok. You know what? I think God might even respond more often when we act like kids than when we act like responsible adults. He alluded to childlike faith. He didn't say take your lifetime of experiences, and roll them around your head for a few minutes, and then approach a relationship with Him from that perspective. Childlike faith; that's one of the key's to operating supernaturally.

Nick's approach changed my way of thinking, and after a few seconds of watching him I started doing the same thing. Just having fun, and releasing the presence of God, and not worrying about what words to use, or what the people around us might think. While I was watching, the Lord gave me an image of a father sitting in a recliner in his living room with a few small children playing on the floor in front of him. The father was proud to see his kids playing, and sharing together, and it brought him happiness. If acting like a kid makes God happy, that is exactly what I am going to do. At one point during the conference we went out into the lobby, and saw a group of people waiting in line to get into the auditorium for the service that was starting 20 minutes later. We decided they must be hungry if they were lined up early, so we went to work. It wasn't long before bodies starting hitting the floor, and we even gave a dose of joy to a random person just passing by; she laughed for a long time after that encounter. We made a bit of a mess in the lobby during that whacking session as people were scattered on the floor blocking part of the entrance. It was a lot of fun, and I felt like a little kid on a playground sharing what God had given to me. Those few moments set the precedent for the rest of that week as we continued looking for people to whack before, and after each service, and it also set the tone for the rest of my life to act like a kid.

Here's the deal. Christianity was never designed to be boring. It was designed to be exciting. When did partnering with God become construed as a mundane, or boring existence? Did the disciples get bored after a few weeks of traveling with Jesus? Of course not; no one could ever grow tired of seeing miracles every day. Most people would jump at the opportunity to meet a President, or other powerful leader simply because of the position of authority they hold. The possibility of eating lunch with the leader of a nation would be exhilarating, so shouldn't we approach our relationship with the one who created everything at least from the same perspective? You should be so excited every time you encounter God that it is difficult to contain your emotions. I think about a child being picked up from daycare. Exhilarated, excited, and jumping up, and down when they catch a glimpse of their parents coming around the corner. And then they run into the arms of their waiting mother, or father. That should be our approach to our relationship with God. That should be our approach when we have the opportunity to pray for someone in need. Not because we just think God might back up what we pray, but because we have confidence in what he said he would do.

Kids have a lot of confidence in what their parents tell them. They don't start thinking mom, and dad are weird, wrong, or crazy until they grow a little older. When they are still young, they have a sense of trust in everything their parents tell them. A two year old child doesn't question dad's ability to protect him. Of course, they ask questions about everything. But they don't wonder if playing on the playground is safe. They don't question whether, or not mom's cooking is healthy. They don't think about the possibility of not having anything to eat. They have complete confidence in everything their parents say, and are at peace with the idea that everything they need in life is available, and will be provided by their parents. Their reality is grounded in trusting their parents. But as we grow older, and start to learn about the harsh realities of the world we live in, and a little bit of insecurity starts to creep into our minds. We start to worry about success, and failure, we become afraid of the darkness, the jungle gym we used to approach fearlessly now seems to be a little too high, and reckless abandon is replaced with cautious trepidation. The complete confidence we used to have is shattered into tiny pieces. And we never really recover. We end up going through the rest of our lives acting like adults in every situation. And that's just silly. Sometimes it's ok to act like a kid. As we go through life we need to walk with the confidence that we know who God is, and who we are, so nothing can phase our approach to the world. This is the type of confidence that enables us to change the world, and gives us the ability to share everything we have experienced.

Sharing is probably a kid's second favorite thing to do besides playing. They love to show off the frog they found in the garden, the painting of the seven legged horse they drew at school, or their new found ability to snap their fingers. They share from their discovery experiences because everything is new to them. Everything is a discovery. There is so much for a child to learn as they discover the world they live in, and it is exciting for them to share those discoveries with others. Truth be told, we do the same thing as adults. Have you ever tasted something you didn't like, and then offered it to someone else? "Hey this is gross; taste it!" Discovery doesn't end when we grow up, it should continue for our entire lives as we approach each new day, and each new experience as an adventure to learn something new. We should approach our relationship with God in the same way. If all the books in the world cannot contain what Jesus did while he walked on the earth[2] than it's a certainty that there is so much more of God that we don't know about. I think it's logical to assume that we will never discover all that God has, or all that he is, during our human lifetime, but that doesn't mean we shouldn't seek all that he has. Moses never had the opportunity to enter the Promised Land, but he still led the Israelites in that direction up until the point of his death. Every new day should be a day to discover more about God, and as we make new discoveries we should share those with others because spiritual hunger is birthed from sharing spiritual experiences.

Being a kid is really just about having fun, and I have learned that you can't hang out with God, and not have fun. Healing the sick is fun! Actually, it's probably the most fun I ever have; especially when it happens in random places like at barbeques, or in airports. Watching God supernaturally rearrange a person's life by healing a wound, or disease they have been struggling with for many years is incredibly exciting. And watching that happen on a regular basis makes the simple act of walking out the front door an exciting, and anticipatory event. I said earlier that Christianity was never designed to be boring; seeing supernatural events will definitely keep you from getting bored. All it takes is one time, and you will be hooked for life. We took a friend with us one day to help with street ministry because she was excited about praying for people, and wanted to see what God would do. The goal was to find people to pray for, and bring them the healing that they needed. She had never seen anyone healed, and although it was something she had heard us talk about, it was not something she ever personally experienced. She had never prayed for anyone, and seen them miraculously healed. It wasn't long after we setup the location that people began coming over to receive free drinks, and in most cases, free prayer. It takes a lot of risk to pray for someone specifically so that they get healed. When you tell someone God can heal them, you are putting yourself in a potentially embarrassing position, because if they don't get healed, you might look a little foolish. Well, there's no might about it, it's pretty much a forgone conclusion that you will look foolish. So it takes some risk to put yourself out there with the hope that a miracle will occur. And I think the risk is even higher within the walls of the church. On the streets there's a pretty good likelihood that you will never see the person you minister to again, so if nothing happens it's not as big of a reputation blow. But in a church where you see the same people every week, you are certain to end up becoming the topic of conversation. This is true if you see people healed, and if you don't. This is true when some people get healed, and others stay sick. There are a lot of variables to supernatural ministry, and some church goers will invariably latch onto the failures more often than the successes.

If you seek miracles to increase your own reputation you will most likely end up doing the exact opposite.

The risk you take could put you in the uncomfortable position of being talked about. Now this could be good, or bad, or both. When God starts performing miracles through you, people will inevitably take notice, and you will become a conversation piece. That's perfectly fine as long as God is getting the glory. If you seek miracles to increase your own reputation you will most likely end up doing the exact opposite. But if people want to talk about what God is doing through you, it gives God the glory he deserves. Another possibility is that people will talk about you when someone is not healed. Those conversations usually stem from a misunderstanding of the will of God. We'll take up that topic later in the book, but for now just know that there is a little risk involved in taking risk. The difference is that when you take risk for God, the only reputation on the line is his. You are taking the risk that he is going to show up, and do what he said. If he doesn't show up the blame can't fall to you. Actually if you look at it from that perspective, the risk is nothing more than a perception. The problem is that we don't teach risk taking in churches. We want everything to be, orderly, and controlled all the time. We're afraid of what might happen if we step out in faith. Or maybe we are concerned about nothing happening at all. Fear of failure can quickly kill a risk taking attitude.

Most churches don't teach how to pray for the sick, and really don't pursue healing. Even many of the charismatic churches that believe in healing rarely go for a miracle because, when you have never seen one, it's hard to imagine one actually happening. I think the reason why there is a resistance to teaching about healing is because the leadership is afraid of how to approach what to do when someone is not healed. That doesn't mean that they don't pray when people are sick. But in the instances where they do step out, and take a little risk, there is so much unbelief that they don't even bother to ask the sick person if they feel better. Imagine if you went to the doctor for cataract surgery, and after the operation they didn't ask you if your sight had improved. Wouldn't that be a little silly? If a doctor never follows up with a patient, there is no way to know if the surgery was a success. There has to be some form of feedback, and discussion to determine if the new state of the patient is better than the previous state. Prayer is no different. If you pray for someone you should ask them how they feel. That's what Jesus did. He encountered a blind man in Mark 8[3], and after praying, he asked him if he could see anything. I think the reason that the question is rarely asked in churches is because there is no real expectation of healing. If you have never seen anyone healed before, it is logical to expect that nothing is going to happen, so there is no point in asking the question. But that is a skewed perspective. That's a perspective that doesn't take God at his word. That's a perspective that doesn't operate with childlike faith.

Jesus said we need to be like children. I've focused partially on how to act like a kid in the sense of being playful, sharing, and daring, but that statement also has an element of believing. Faith is a huge currency in heaven. Hebrews 11[4] shows us that it is impossible to please God if we don't have any faith. If you are a Christian, you have faith. You had to have faith to accept Jesus as the Messiah, and you continue in that faith by continuing in the lifestyle of a Christian. Childlike faith believes that what he told you is true. Childlike faith believes that you can do what he said. But as we grow up we lose that ability to be imaginative as we allow the reality of the physical world around us to color what we believe. We should really be living from the perspective that everything in the Bible is true, and that when we apply it to our lives through the lens of childlike faith it supersedes the physical reality allowing us to live a miraculous lifestyle. We are all called to live from that perspective. In Matthew 6^5, in the famous model prayer, Jesus used the phrase "on earth as it is in heaven." That is the correct perspective; making earth look like heaven by continuing what Jesus started through the release of God's love. Healing the sick is part of that perspective. Whacking, and stacking is part of it too. Living like a child can go a long way towards accomplishing the goals of heaven.

Now let's get back to our friend, and our street ministry time. We probably prayed for about 40 people that day, and saw 25 of them healed during just a few hours. And this person who never saw anyone healed when she prayed, was amazed that God healed at least five people through her hands. She was ruined for life. She got a taste of the supernatural, and spent the rest of the day excited about what God had done. What do kids do when they find something new that they like? They latch onto it! Have you ever seen a kid watch the same movie every day? They watch it so often that they know every word, and yet there is still a sense of excitement, and anticipation as their favorite scene comes to the screen. Why would anyone want to experience the same exact thing every day? When you find something you really love, it's hard to let it go. We all do this. We have a favorite pair of jeans, favorite color, best friends, and probably something we like the most in just about every category of life. It's normal to keep the things we like close by. So what if you could have the things of God close by? What if healing was always within arm's length? What if miraculous events were literally sitting on the tips of your fingers just waiting to be passed onto someone in need? I think that is something we would all want to latch onto.

So that's my view on becoming like little children. When we approach God from the perspective of a child we cannot help, but believe in everything he said. The experiences written on the pages of the Bible were not just for the people who lived two thousand years ago. They are for everyone who believes. But belief requires us to unlearn, so that we can then relearn. We have to unlearn the ideas of what is impossible, and relearn the reality that anything is possible. Now, I don't want to confuse childlike faith with mindless obedience. God doesn't want an army of mindless robots. He gave us intelligence for a purpose, but he also doesn't want the intelligence to supersede his word. His reality is a higher reality than our own, and we have to approach that reality through the eyes of a child, that has the imagination to see what is missing, and then has the faith to take hold of it. If I told you to imagine reaching your hand up to heaven, and pulling down something you need, could you do it? A child could. If I told you that you could reach into heaven, and pull down a brand new lung for someone who needs it, would you believe me? A child would. A child could picture in their mind what they wanted, and then take hold of it through their imagination. The reality is this, if you have to become like little children to enter the kingdom of heaven, certainly you have to act like a kid to access everything in that kingdom.

Endnotes
1. Matthew 18:3
2. John 21:25
3. Mark 8:24
4. Hebrews 11:6
5. Matthew 6:10

Going Deeper

1. Does the idea of acting like a kid offend you? Why, or why not?

---

2. Does the idea of people becoming overwhelmed with God's presence by falling down, or laughing offend you? Why, or why not?

---

3. Do you struggle with the idea of crossing the line between childlike faith, and irreverence to God? Where do you draw that line?

---

4. Do you believe that you can access anything in God's kingdom through childlike faith?

Deeper Prayer

Faith can be a little crazy sometimes, but just like a muscle, it grows the more we use it. Having childlike faith basically means that we are willing to pray for anything that is in line with what God wants to do on the earth. Here's a prayer you can pray if you want to start praying with more childlike faith:

Daddy, I want to see you as the amazing, loving Father who longs to see his children enjoy the kingdom he created. I want to see life through the eyes of childlike faith, be willing to take any risk you call me to, pray for anything, and anyone you put in my path, and live with an expectation to see my prayers instantly, and miraculously answered. I ask that you renew my sense of wonder about you, and shift my perspective in any area where I have become overly religious, so that I can live with the type of faith, and risk that changes the world.

CHAPTER SIX

RISK

God loves risk takers. He loves it when we step out in faith to accomplish his goals on the earth. It's not easy taking risk. If it was, everyone would do it, and then we would probably call it safety. Risk involves the possibility of failure, and that by itself tends to make people avoid risk, because no one likes to fail. There are formulas for how to avoid risk, and methods of transferring risk to others through insurance policies, but in the kingdom of heaven, risk is less of a danger, and more of a currency. John Wimber, one of the founders of the Vineyard movement, is often quoted as saying "faith is spelled R.I.S.K." If you go back in history, you'll find that risk was a little different for the early apostles who faced the possibility of death for teaching about Jesus. The same is still true in some countries today, though that form of risk has diminished, and only seems to exist in small pockets of the world. The real risk most Christians face today is that of humiliation. We're often afraid that our reputation will be tarnished if we start doing crazy things, like offering miracles to sick people. It's a pretty big risk to stop a stranger on the street, and ask them if they need a miracle. First, because you are going to look a little foolish if a miracle doesn't happen, and second, because they may refuse prayer simply on the grounds that they think you are crazy. But the potential for success in seeing a miracle is what should drive you forward. Don't focus on the possibility of failure. Focus instead on what God said would happen when we pray for the sick. There are two sides to the risk coin. One is failure, and the other is success. Take risk for the chance of success, and don't worry about the other side of the coin.

Several years ago the Lord spoke to me about the ministry he was preparing me for, and he told me that some people would hate me because of what he was calling me to do. That was a tough pill to swallow. He also told me I would lose some of my friends, and that even some members of my family would distance themselves from me. As I look back on that night I realize that I was pretty quick in my response. I was so desperate for more of God that I was willing to lose earthly relationships to follow him anywhere he was leading. I told him I was willing to do whatever it took to be used by him. Those can be dangerous prayers; actually I think they are always dangerous prayers. It's a risky proposition offering up all of yourself to God. God wants us to want to be closer to him, so when we pray from that perspective it's always aligned with his will. And he always responds to that type of prayer. It wasn't much later that some of my closer relationships became strained, and people began to withdraw from me. I would be lying if I told you it didn't upset me. Close friends became distant friends, and though it hurt, it did make it a lot easier to move to the East coast when that time had come. It was like the opening moves of a chess game. I had no idea what God's strategy was, but as each new move was played I found myself in different situations that required me to seriously contemplate the next step I was going to take. There was some hesitation at times as I wasn't always sure where events were going to lead me, but I always knew that God was in control, and the orchestration of his plan was the best way forward.

I think again about Abraham, and how he was called to leave most of his family behind, and risk everything he had to go after what God was putting in front of him. It wasn't very long into the journey before some infighting started, and Abraham had to split off from some of the family that came with him in, order to keep the peace[1]. Abraham took his wife, and belongings with him, of course, but I think taking his nephews family along was not part of God's plan. It's interesting to me that God told Abraham to leave his family, and the ones he didn't leave behind turned into a source of negativity in his life. They ended up peeling away from the group, and later created even more problems that forced Abraham into a war. I wonder how things would have played out if his nephew had stayed behind. It seems that God wanted Abraham alone, so that he wouldn't have any outside influence to color what he was about to show him. That's not to say that all of Abraham's family was evil, but human reasoning will often challenge God's viewpoint. People who are in a position to speak into your life have a great influence over you. I know God removed some people from my life by moving me to the other side of the country; at the time I didn't want to move, but it turned out to be the greatest move I have ever made. The funny thing is that God showed me in a dream that we were about to make a big move eight months before it happened, but I totally misinterpreted what the dream meant. In my dream I saw a large moving truck in front of my house, a crew packing all of our belongings into the truck, there was a little bit of chaos as seems to occur with all moves, and there was a random stranger on a bicycle who stopped by to visit.

I didn't know much about dream interpretation at the time, so I tried to come up with representations for the truck, the chaos, and the other elements of the dream. I put it all I my dream journal, and eventually forgot about it. As we were unpacking in our new home that following year I stopped to skim through my dream journal, and came across what I now refer to as "the moving dream." I was shocked to find out that it wasn't an allegorical dream; it was an actual vision of the future. The events that happened in the dream happened on moving day. What stood out to me the most was that a random stranger rode up on a bicycle, and had a conversation with me while I was helping to load the truck, just like I had seen in the dream. God literally showed me moving day eight months before it occurred; if I had known better I would have been much more prepared for the move. I had become uncomfortable where I was previously satisfied, and God showed me it was time to make a move. God will make us uncomfortable in our surroundings, so that we look to him for guidance on the shift that needs to occur. I'm confident that God always responds anytime a prayer is uttered that voluntarily offers up a life for service. We have no information about Abraham's life before God told him to move, but I have to assume a relationship already existed between this man, and his God. The genealogical accounts in Genesis reveal that Noah was still alive when Abraham was born, and lived for almost 60 more years. There's a good likelihood that Abraham had a relationship with his really old ancestor who God had used to save the human race several hundred years earlier. That would be a powerful influence in anyone's life. God spoke to Abraham, and told him to move, and he obeyed, but I bet there was some hesitation as he told his wife they had to pack up, and move out. Somehow I can picture Sarai giving him a crazy look when she thought about the risk that was involved.

I'm sure some of you think I'm a little crazy, especially if you have never seen any miracles. I have shared some personal stories already, and I'll share a few more as these chapters move along about the encounters I have had with God. These encounters have grounded me in a place of taking risk regardless of how crazy it may make me look to others. Abraham probably looked a little crazy. And Noah definitely looked crazy. I'm not comparing myself to these patriarchs, but I do see a common thread in the lives of Biblical figures, and current day Christian leaders. The ones who are willing to take God directed risk are always given the opportunity to steward over something amazing. And the ones who choose comfort, and stability are rarely placed in the category of history makers. I don't care about fame, but I do want to make history for God. Well, I don't care about fame on earth anyways, but I do want to be famous in heaven, and feared in hell. If my enemy is afraid of me, that means I'm moving in the right direction. When we take risks for God it impacts the kingdom of heaven, and the kingdom of hell. The evil spirits mentioned in Acts 19[2] knew who Paul was because his ministry was impacting their ability to keep people in bondage. Armies always know who the leaders are in the opposing force. The demons knew Paul by name because his work was raining down destruction on their ranks, and destroying their efforts to keep humanity in darkness. I want the demons to know me by name. Not because I want to have some familiarity with them, but because when I walk into a room I want the citizens of hell to freak out. It's been said that the devil will attack those who have an impact on his kingdom. My response to that is this: BRING IT! The reality is that if the devil doesn't know your name, you aren't taking enough risk.

Risk, when in line with the will of God,
will always turn into success.

There's a concept in business that teaches about how to balance risk with reward. A company cannot always avoid risk, risk in some form always has to be accepted because the potential trade off could turn into a financial profit. This is known as speculative risk, and it involves decisions like, buying new machinery, speculating on new products, stocking more inventory, or creating an advertising plan. You generally have to spend money to make it, and in the business world, that always involves the possibility of taking a loss if the venture is unsuccessful. Entrepreneurs take risks every day, and put virtually everything on the line in the hopes that their idea for a business model will be successful. The downside to this is that, in business, risk does not always equal reward. Ideas fall apart, and people can quickly lose their life's savings in a failed attempt at launching a business. The potential for loss is what keeps most people from taking risk. But with God the potential for loss is zero. Risk, when in line with the will of

God, will always turn into success. We can confidently take risk in partnership with God, and know that it will turn into success. This is why Hebrews 11[3] says that "faith is confidence in what we hope for, and assurance about what we do not see." It is confidence in knowing that the thing we are pursuing is going to happen. That could be in the area of any type of ministry whether it is healing, church planting, counseling, etc. God wants partners who are willing to take risk because it shows our faith that we expect him to show up, and play an active role in the partnership. God could have spoken a boat into existence for Noah, and his family. He could have even changed their DNA, so that they could have gills, and breathe under water. But he instead told Noah to build the boat[4]. He knew Noah would look crazy, but he wanted a partner who was willing to risk even his reputation for the purpose of serving God. People who don't take risks, rarely make a major impact on the world, or even on their own lives. Following God is all about risk.

As I began to push into this new lifestyle of ministry I started to research others who have taken greater risks than I have yet to do, and who see amazing miracles everywhere they go. I have learned that examining what God has done in others' lives, and learning from their ministry experiences can go a long way in helping to understand how to partner with God, and it builds a lot of faith along the way. Gleaning from their wisdom has taught me more than I ever could have learned otherwise. Some think the church has gone through cycles of inactivity in regards to the miraculous with just a few resurgences over the years, but there has actually been very few, if any, periods of inactivity since Jesus showed up[5]. There have also been major revivals that brought a great outpouring of God's power, and I'd like to examine the lives of some of those who put it all on the line, with the hope that God would show up, and show off. Lots of books have already been written about the revivalists, and evangelists of the early, and mid-1900's, but there are a few people today who have taken a large risk in reaching the lost with supernatural ministries. They are modern day pioneers that are expanding the kingdom of heaven every day, and their stories are absolutely amazing.

 Heidi, and Rolland Baker see dead people come back to life. Yeah, you read that correctly; dead people who aren't dead anymore. That's pretty amazing! It didn't start out that way, but in 1995 they felt God prompting them to move to Mozambique where they took over operation of a rundown, orphanage already teeming with children that nobody wanted to care for. Ministry wasn't a foreign topic to these two risk takers. They had already been ministering for more than a decade to the poor in Asia, and England, and they jumped at the opportunity to head into what was then the poorest nation in the world. The culture in Mozambique can be devastating for anyone who is sick, or unwanted. Sadly, it was common to see kids dying on the dirt streets because the parents were dead, or worse, just didn't want them anymore. This was true for adults as well who were unable to care for themselves, and had no one else willing to take care of their needs. It's a sad reality of what happens in a society that is so devastated by guerilla warfare, witchcraft, poverty, and destitution that the people stop caring for themselves, or each other. One year into Heidi, and Rolland's mission, with the, orphanage in much better shape, and with over 300 kids to care for, the government decided to shut them down. But that didn't deter what God was doing. It wasn't easy trying to care for these children without a facility, but the Lord always came through, and a few months after the government shut them down, a more permanent location was donated that continues to function today as a spring of life for children in need. Today they serve the needs of more than 10,000 children in 15 countries, operate several Bible, and primary schools, and oversee a network of 10,000 churches in the region. They have endured government intimidation, stoning's, and even the threat of contract killings. Add to this that they both became seriously ill, and were later miraculously healed, all after moving to Mozambique. And through it all, they have faithfully persisted to share God's love to those in need regardless of the risk involved[6].

I love Heidi's model of evangelism. She will boldly walk into a village, and declare that she is there to heal the sick by essentially demanding someone bring her a deaf person. Imagine you are sitting in your back yard, and a lady walks up, and demands you bring out someone who is deaf, or blind. How do you respond to that? The villagers will often respond by bringing someone to her, and God will miraculously heal them on the spot. And the next thing you know their having church in the dirt as people learn about Jesus, give their lives to him, and many more are miraculously healed. That's one way to grow the Church, and it sounds a lot like what Jesus did. Stroll into town, heal some sick people, and share the good news. I'm thinking there's probably not a better method. But there is one other exciting twist to the story. Just as Jesus sent his disciples out to heal the sick, Heidi, and Rolland bring some of the kids from the children's home along with them to these villages. They aren't just there to play with the other kids, or put on a show, they are the ministry team. The kids pray for the sick, and God does amazing things through them. Jesus said in Matthew 19[7] "Let the little children come to me, and do not hinder them, for the kingdom of heaven belongs to such as these." They have taken that statement literally, and put the kids at work in the ministry of healing. And it's not just deaf ears. If you can think of a sickness, they have probably seen it healed. Quadriplegics, and paraplegics have walked again, the blind have received their eyesight, and yeah, the dead have come back to life.

Another missionary I greatly admire is Leif Hetland. Leif spent some time in Africa as well, and has seen many miracles there as well as in the 78 other nations he has ministered in. Over one million people have come to Christ through his ministry. One million lives have been changed because this man, and his wife chose to take some big risks in parts of the world where their lives were literally on the line. It was in Pakistan where he has taken the most risk, and God has given amazing breakthrough as a result; more than 500,000 Muslims have changed their faith after seeing God work through Leif. Pakistan is considered by many to be the most spiritually dark place on earth. It is a predominantly Muslim nation where 95% of the residents practice some form of Islam, and it has been a historically dangerous place for Christians. But none of that deterred Leif from taking the message of Jesus to the Muslims, all because of love. He would purchase space on billboards advertising the miracles that were going to occur knowing that his chances of leaving alive were slim if Jesus didn't show up. But he still went because God's love is stronger than anyone else's hatred. He talks about this type of love in one of his books[8], "I am a lover, and I will forever stay a lover. It is not only my identity, it is my responsibility. When others want to talk about doctrine, I want to talk about the Father's love. When others want to talk about morality, I want to talk about the Father's love. When others want to talk about politics, I want to talk about the Father's love."

Like Heidi, and Roland, Leif takes the approach of representing Jesus by doing exactly what he preaches. He demonstrates what he teaches by declaring healing into people's lives, and he has estimated that 90% of the salvations they have seen are a result of people being healed. He has seen crowds of Muslims shouting praise after Jesus recreated every deteriorated muscle of a quadriplegic that then climbed out of his chair, and began to walk. Salvation follows miracles; you can't avoid being impacted when Jesus heals you. I grew up in church, I have spent my whole life in church, and I have heard thousands of salvation messages, and even after hearing some of the greatest sermons, the number of the people who responded have been extremely small compared to what is seen in services where miracles occur. I know angels rejoice over each soul that is saved, but we have an opportunity to see so many more lives touched. There is something about the supernatural that gets people excited, and makes them want to be involved. I'm laser focused on miracles because I've seen the impact it has, not just on the people who are touched, but also on their friends, and families who experience the miracle second hand. Salvation is still the greatest miracle of all, but I know that one often leads to the other, and if I can introduce a broken person to Jesus, and see them made physically, and spiritually whole, it's a great combination.

***If you want to see God move in powerful ways you
are going to have to start taking some risks.***

There are more people being healed, and set free from oppression today than any other time in church history. It is happening in every country of the world, but it is happening the least in North America. Why are more people being healed on the African continent, or in Asia than in the nation where most of the world's missionaries have, originated from? I think the answer is that we need more people taking risk right here at home. God wants all of us to be involved in what he is doing, and anyone who is willing to step out, and take some risk can be part of the team God uses to heal the world. It's not enough to mail a check off to a missionary, or be part of a passive prayer chain. If you want to see God move in powerful ways, you are going to have to start taking some risks. You might look foolish, but remember what Jesus told us in Matthew 5[9], "Blessed are you when people insult you, persecute you, and falsely say all kinds of evil against you because of me. Rejoice, and be glad, because great is your reward in heaven, for in the same way they persecuted the prophets who were before you." Faith can look like foolishness to the eyes of someone who isn't a risk taker. Let's be realistic, risk takers in the church are often misunderstood, because they are usually all alone. My faith isn't based on how many people are with me, or what other people think. Jesus said we are the light of the world, and I am going to let that light shine everywhere I go. And I'll tell you something else; the more risk I take, the easier it gets. It used to be hard to flip on the supernatural light switch, but now it's just a natural expression of God's love. I know who I am, I know who he is, and I know his heart. So I can operate from the perspective of knowing what he has already done, and that he wants to do more of the same. And because I know his heart, the risk becomes a lot easier, because the expectation of the results is much greater.

I might look a little crazy when I chase down someone using crutches, but what looks crazy to me is the other 200 Christians who walk right past the crutches, and ignore the person leaning on them. Come on! Don't be overwhelmed by the circumstance of the person standing in front of you. Instead, be overwhelmed by the power of the one you represent. The creator of the universe has given you the authority to eliminate every kind of sickness. It doesn't matter what it is, or why it is there. But to eliminate sickness you have to go after it. If you never pray for anyone, no one will ever be healed. I don't ever want to be in the position of walking past someone in need when I know I carry the very thing that can make them whole. The possibility of a life being changed makes any, and all risk worth it. There really is no greater reward than to see someone who was on crutches celebrate by running around a building, or someone who was deaf explore the audio environment they have been missing out on for the very first time. God has expected his partners to take risk from the beginning of time. Take the risk. You'll be glad that you did.

Endnotes
1. Gen 13:7-11
2. Acts 19:15
3. Hebrews 11:1
4. Genesis 6:14
5. 2000 Years of charismatic Christianity by Eddie L. Hyatt
6. There is Always Enough by Heidi, and Rolland Baker
7. Matthew 19:14
8. Seeing through heaven's eyes: A worldview that will transform your life by Leif Hetland.
9. Matthew 5:11-12

Going Deeper

1. How much does taking risk scare you?

---

2. Are you willing to take any level of risk, if it means you will see miraculous results?

---

3. Are you willing to take any level of risk, even if the miraculous result doesn't happen?

---

4. Do you think the risk taken by believers today is more, or less than the risk Jesus' disciples took?

Deeper Prayer

Most people are not born with a risk taking attitude, and you may be thinking that this risk taking lifestyle is not for you. It can be a little scary at first, but I guarantee you that, if you are willing to take risk, God will start showing up more often. It may not be on the first try, but eventually, you will start to see miraculous results. When God knows he can trust you to pray for the sick, he will start flowing his power through you. When he knows he can trust you with his secrets, he will start to share those secrets with you. It really does flow from your relationship with him. Here's a great risk taking declaration and prayer for you:

I declare today that I am a risk taker for Jesus. I have been created to change the world, and I will take whatever risk is required of me by Jesus to see the world transformed. Jesus, help me to have so much love for everyone I encounter that I will be willing to take any amount of risk to show them your love in whatever way they need it. I long to see your kingdom impact this earth, and I want to be a major part of what you are doing today. Let me be famous in heaven, and feared in hell because of the risk I take for you.

CHAPTER SEVEN

MANDATE

"Heal the sick, raise the dead, cleanse those who have leprosy, drive out demons.[1]" That's the mandate Jesus gave to the disciples as part of their instructions when he sent them out on a mission. And it's a pretty powerful mandate because prior to that, we don't see any disciples operating in that realm. Even the disciples had to take some risk, and step out in faith to minister, without Jesus standing next to them. I've mentioned that verse at least once so far in this book, but I want to go back, and spend some time really unpacking what it means. This was the mission Jesus gave to his disciples not long after they started working together. He gave another 72 disciples a similar mandate in Luke 10, and then just before leaving earth he made this final statement[2]: "And these signs will accompany those who believe: In my name they will drive out demons; they will speak in new tongues...they will place their hands on sick people, and they will get well."

Any mandate Jesus gave to his disciples applies to us because we are also his disciples. A disciple is a follower so even though we may not have walked down a dusty road with him a few thousand years ago, we are certainly continuing, today, the mission he started on earth. Paul wasn't part of the, original 12 disciples, or of the additional 72, and yet, we see several examples in the scriptures of God performing miracles through him, including raising someone from the dead. Ananias, the one who prayed for Paul after his famous encounter with Jesus[3] also wasn't mentioned anywhere as an, original disciple of Christ. And yet Paul's eyes were healed when Ananias prayed for him. Jesus said John the Baptist was the greatest Old Testament prophet, but that the least in the kingdom of heaven is greater than John[4]. That's you. Well, maybe not the least part, but you are definitely part of the kingdom of heaven. So at the very least, every Christian today carries a status equal to the disciples, and the apostles that we see mentioned in scripture. That means that you have the same mandate the disciples were given. I could try to put a guilt trip on you, and tell you to just go do what you were told, but that wouldn't be very effective, so let's instead take a look at the current state of Christianity, and why what we consider to be normal today, is not the same normal other believers have experienced.

    Every church seems to be a little different, and when you move as often as I have, you always end up in a situation where you try to find a "good" church to attend. This is generally subjective based on your own needs; some are looking for a good children's ministry while others might be more concerned with a particular style of worship. We try to find a church that matches our interests, and beliefs because we want to be comfortable, and fit in like we did in our previous church. I find it interesting how we pick a church based on what we believe, and that we even tend to pick, and choose what we want to believe, and more importantly, what we want to follow. The Bible isn't a book of suggestions where you can pick, and choose the parts you like, and toss out everything else. I'll use tithing as an example because it's something we can all relate to. All Christians know what tithing is, we know that God has given us a mandate to cheerfully give a percentage of our income back to him so that the Church can function. But not everyone tithes. Now we'll come up with lots of excuses about how we don't like the way the church is spending the money, or about how the pastor's car is a little too nice, or maybe even that the last sermon hit a little too close to home. Or maybe your finances are so tight that it's too difficult to give. Regardless of the reason, it's easy to make excuses about what we don't want to do when it impacts the way we live. Tithing is a simple example, but there are so many other areas of our walk where we do the same thing.

I also find it interesting that we make up our own mandates that God never required of us. I remember in the 1980's a lot of churches taught that going to the movies was a sin. They didn't care what the rating was, if you went to the movie theater, you were a sinner. You also have the churches that say women should never wear makeup, or pants, and their dresses always have to be of ankle length. I know, these are pretty extreme examples, but I want to make a point here. We make stuff up for silly reasons. I'm sure they had a Bible verse to loosely base their moral concerns from, but their misrepresentations of God's word pushed a lot of people away. Even today, I hear stories all the time about people who don't go to church because they were mistreated in the church. I hear stories about churches that refuse to pray for you if they don't have a record of your tithing. Your kid could be dying in the hospital, and the first thing they do is check the database to make sure you are all paid up. This is not the church that Jesus came to earth, and sacrificed his life for; this is religion, and there is a big difference. When we choose what we want to do, and impose our own personal viewpoints on others as if they are God's viewpoints, we're not representing him, we're representing religion. The spirit of religion is destroying the church, and it's time to kick it out for good! How can anyone expect to see God bless what they are doing when their actions are hurting the very people they are supposed to be helping? Jesus encountered this same attitude in his day which is probably why he appeared crass when dealing with the religious leaders. I wonder how Jesus would address the leaders of some of our churches today. Here's the reality, if your walk doesn't transform you "into his image with ever-increasing glory, which comes from the Lord[5]" than you're either moving in the wrong direction, or you have ended up on a plateau like I did.

The point is this, we have churches doing some ridiculous stuff; stupid really. And then we have churches that are "normal" because they don't do what these extreme pastors are doing. And then we have churches where miracles happen every day. All of the spectrums are covered. Some denominations don't believe miracles are for today, actively teach against that concept, and go after pastors, and congregation members within their, organization who do. Other denominations believe miracles are possible, but never actually see any occur. God never intended to have thousands of denominations with hundreds of different interpretations of his word. His plan wasn't to have a fractured Church that competes with each other, but that is exactly what we have become. I read an article a few years ago about how the Pope was concerned over the number of Catholics in South America who were leaving Catholicism to join other denominations. Jesus didn't show up on earth, and tell John the Baptist to start one denomination, and then Peter to start another; he actually prayed in John 17[6] that we would all be one. The problem is that we are not all moving in the same direction. We're more concerned about the size, or look of our local church than we are about the mandate Jesus has given us. I love big churches, and I love that they are able to reach so many people every week, but if the focus of the ministry is on the inside of the walls, they have missed the point of Jesus' message. It's one thing to build a building, and wait for people to come to you. It's another thing entirely to go out into the communities, find those in need, and give them the answer to their problems. We need both of those focuses for sure, but we can't take the approach that one church works on the community while another serves the needs of its members. We all need to be moving in the same direction.

Really I think the Church as a whole is a bit off course. We're not far off course, but we have been off course for a long time. Think about this; if an airplane starts out heading just one degree off course, over time that one degree can lead the pilot hundreds of miles away from the intended destination. It's a simple issue to fix, if a course correction is made early on, but if it goes unnoticed it will create a big problem near the end of the flight. I think the state of Christianity today shows us that we have been off course for a long time. God has, orchestrated a few course corrections over the centuries, but they have only come when believers decided to take God at his word, and follow what he has mandated us to do. Martin Luther made a big shift in 1517 when he hammered his ninety-five thesis to the door of the church. That was a huge course correction that brought about the protestant reformation, and ultimately led to what we have today. As a side note, my wife is a direct descendant of Martin Luther, and I have a revolution minded ancestor in my lineage as well; the famous Daniel Boone who fought in the American Revolutionary War, and led explorations of, what we now know as, the State of Kentucky. We feel like one of the reasons we are so passionate about reformation, and revolution within the church is because it is literally in our blood. I see Martin Luther's actions as the first step in a series of moves God made to pave the way for a new outpouring of his Spirit on earth. What happened to the disciples in the upper room should have never ended, but somewhere between that day, and Martin Luther's day, we lost our focus. There were a handful of people peppered throughout the centuries that believed, and operated in the gifts of the Holy Spirit, but they were few, and far between, and none led to major revivals, or movements like the ones that have occurred in the past few hundred years. Another course correction came with the Azusa Street revival in Los Angeles in the early 1900's. For three years people of all races, and denominations gathered in a little building on a daily basis to experience an outpouring of God's presence that probably hadn't been seen, or at least recorded, since the activities in the upper room many years earlier. Martin Luther birthed Protestantism, and Azusa Street rebirthed Pentecostalism. Over the next century a handful of other revivalist ministers were used by God to continue moving us back towards where we should have been all along. People like John Alexander Dowie, John G. Lake, William Branham, Kathryn Kuhlman, Lester Sumrall, A.A. Allen, Smith Wigglesworth, Aimee Semple McPherson, and John Wimber are just a few of those who continued to steward a move of God, and a lifestyle of miracles throughout the 20th century. And in 1994 another revival, led by Randy Clark, broke out in Toronto, Canada that birthed, or reenergized several major ministries that continue to impact the world for the kingdom of God today.

How about we just do what the Bible says, and pattern our lives after Jesus?

The point I'm trying to make here is that when the believers get together, and do what Jesus did amazing things start to happen. When we make the decision to be obedient to the mandate we have been given, God shows up in amazing ways. So here's a crazy idea, how about we just do what the Bible says, and pattern our lives after Jesus? I know it's a pretty wild notion, but stick with me on this for a minute. Jesus had a couple of really simple mandates. He basically said to love people, treat them the way you want to be treated, and oh yeah, go heal the sick, and raise the dead. So why do churches teach about the love part, and ignore the supernatural stuff? Do we only have a partial gospel? Is the good news still good if we leave out some of the best stuff? You can love people, but if you don't have what they need, you can't help them with anything. Almost anyone would stop on the side of the road to help someone in an accident, but only someone with medical training could provide a professional level of assistance to help with physical injuries. Anyone else might cause more damage because they don't have the skills, or abilities to render the proper aid. This is the picture of a weak church. There are a lot of people who are willing to love, but don't have the power to bring change. They love enough to go visit you in the hospital, but they can't get you out of the hospital.

That isn't the complete gospel. You can't embrace the cross for salvation, and ignore the power it provides to live supernaturally. It's all connected, but sadly the majority of believers would rather be comfortable, than accept the responsibility of doing what Jesus instructed. It's not just about getting into heaven; it's about bringing heaven to earth. Jesus brought a complete gospel, and when we follow his model it will transform our lives, and the lives of others into his image.

One thing my military career trained me on is how to be good at following, orders. Maybe this is why we see military analogies weaved into the scriptures. We had a saying that the military doesn't practice democracy, we protect it. That's a true statement, because regardless of the branch of service, everyone's basic role is to carry out the, orders of the person above them. Whether you have one stripe, or four stars on your uniform, you have a boss who gives you direction, and you quickly learn that there's not always room for discussion. I wasn't always the best at following, orders in the military. Just like most other young members, I challenged some authority early on, and learned through various measures, that doing what the boss says, even when you don't agree with it, or don't understand why it has to be done that way, is part of the structure of a military environment. If soldiers stopped to argue on the battlefield every time an, order was given, the enemy would easily decimate our forces, and decisively win the battle. Naturally, churches can't be structured like military, organizations because that would create a whole new level of problems. But we do have an obligation to follow the direction of the Holy Spirit as he issues our, orders. Jesus said in John 14[7] "if you love me, you will keep my commands." That seems pretty simple to a military guy who is used to following, orders, so maybe that's why when I see verses that say love your neighbor as yourself, or heal the sick I take them at face value as mandates, not recommendations, or suggestions. If your goal is to live fully for God, you have to be willing to accept the direction he has given.

Jesus quoted a passage from Isaiah in Matthew 13[8] when he was explaining to the disciples why he spoke to them plainly while speaking to others in parables. It was a harsh description of the people of that day, and his explanation seems a lot like a description of today's church. We have allowed our own hearts to become calloused, and as a result we are not able to see, or hear what God is doing. Callouses on the skin are built up over time, and keep us from feeling pain, or discomfort from some activities. I play the guitar every now, and then for fun, and I remember how painful it was when I first started playing; pressing down on those thin metal strings over, and over really hurt. As time went on the skin on my fingertips began to thicken as callouses formed where the fingers had repeated contact with the strings. My body was creating a method of protection to eliminate future injury, or soreness. Now when I play the guitar, I can feel the pressure of the stings against my fingers, but it doesn't hurt anymore. You could say that I have built up a resistance to thin metal strings. Something similar happens to our hearts as we go through life. God speaks, and we ignore him. He speaks again, and we choose not to listen. Over time we grow resistant to the move of the Holy Spirit, and eventually we stop noticing when he shows up because our heart doesn't feel it anymore. Here's the deal, God is still speaking to us, but we may have stopped listening. When we stop listening, it eventually forms callouses that harden our hearts to his will. The disciples quickly responded when Jesus told them to follow him, and by the time they reached the point of Matthew 13, they had already seen miracles happen through their own hands, so it would have been difficult for them not to listen a little closer. Verse 17[9] of this same chapter says "many prophets, and righteous people longed to see what you see, but did not see it, and to hear what you hear, but did not hear it." The prophets were the closest people to God in the Old Testament; they were the ones who delivered God's message to the kings, and to the rest of the people, and yet Jesus said that even they didn't have a chance to see what the disciples could. Why? Because a shift had occurred when the Messiah showed up, and a new authority was made available to believers. So many people in Jesus' time, as well as today, continued to resist the reality of that authority, and as a result, they were kept from seeing, hearing, or understanding their new role. And it seems to me that, in most churches, it is the men who seem to be the most calloused, and the most resistant.

My wife and I led a small group for a few years for the church we attend where we taught about how to live a supernatural lifestyle. The group was made up of mostly women. We had a lot of interest from men, and women when we first launched the group, but most of the men never showed up when they learned about the topics we would be discussing, and the goals we had set. We only had one guy that first time besides me, and then it doubled to two in the second term, but the men were still greatly outnumbered. Sadly, that didn't shock me, because it seems to be the norm. Guys are quick to jump into ministry that involves building a house, or doing some yard work, but ask them to sit on a couch, and discuss their feelings about God, and they run, and hide. This isn't meant to be an attack on men; there are plenty of women who avoid these discussions as well. The unfortunate reality is that a lot of people aren't ready to take that next step of what God has planned for all of us. A calloused heart will keep you from moving forward because you can't clearly see what the next step needs to be. This causes that comfortableness I talked about earlier. This is what leads you to a plateau where you think you're in a good place, but what has really happened is you have stalled in your growth, and have settled into a comfortable routine. And the worst part is that you're not even aware of it. I was there too, and I didn't have a clue that I had fallen into the same trap. If this resonates with you, set this book down right now, and ask God to remove the callouses from your heart. You can't move any further if you can't see, or hear the directions. Take a minute to think about whether, or not you are comfortable. Jesus has given you a mandate; you're either following the mandate, or you've fallen into the trap. There's not any in between ground here, it's one, or the other. And the Church cannot be, what it needs to be to the world, until we start following everything we have been mandated to do.

Later in Matthew 13[10], Jesus also shared that the seed that falls on good soil will bear fruit to varying degrees of "a hundred, sixty, or thirty times what was sown." The first thing I notice here is that a seed in good soil always produces fruit, but it doesn't always produce the same amount. If the soil is good, something will grow, but the amount that grows is determined by the one who stewards the seed. If a farmer plants a large field full of seeds, and only waters it once each week, the crop he reaps is going to be much less than if he watered it as often as needed. The seed that doesn't get a lot of water is not going to produce a plant large enough to sustain an abundance of fruit. I noticed this in my own garden where the tomato plants that received more water produced five times the amount of fruit than the others. Once the seed is planted in us we have to steward it to make it grow. I used to think that every generation would have one, or two people who were called by God to be used for powerful purposes on earth, and that they were the special ones God set apart for healing, and other supernatural ministries. If we look at history, and the few people I mentioned earlier, I think that's exactly what we see on the surface. But when I think about that in the context of this verse I see another possibility. Perhaps those who were mightily used by God were the ones who stewarded the seed to the point that their yield of fruit was much larger than everyone else's. They took a look at Jesus' words in Mark 16[11], and grabbed hold of the reality that Jesus was describing. They chose to believe in the supernatural elements of Christianity. I realize today that everyone can be used in this same way. Anyone who is willing to steward the seed God has placed within them will produce more fruit. We will be known by our fruits; I don't know about you, but if I have a choice to produce a little, or a lot, I'm going to choose a lot every day of the week. And by the way, we won't get to do any of this stuff in heaven. Your only chance to heal the sick, or raise the dead is while you walk on this earth; once your life is over that opportunity is gone.

We only have a short amount of time to really have fun with partnering with God in this way.

"Heal the sick, raise the dead…,[12]" that's your mandate. That's the mandate for all Christians. Unfortunately, unless you're a senior leader in your church, you likely won't be able to fully put this newfound knowledge into immediate practice within a church service. You can't go into your church tomorrow, and try to change everything all at once. And you shouldn't try either. I learned a long time ago that change comes slowly, and a comfortable church will need to be slowly moved in the right direction. Unless, of course, revival breaks out, and then they will either jump in head first, or leave, and never come back. But you can't go to your pastors, and tell him everything needs to change, because quite honestly, they would probably be offended, or upset that you don't think they are leading the church in the right direction. Instead, find a place to serve where you can apply this mandate, and start seeing lives changed. If you're not afforded the opportunity to go for miracles in the church, go find sick people somewhere else. God will honor it. I actually see more miracles outside the walls of the church than I do inside. Not because people in the church don't get healed, but because I try to look for opportunities everywhere I go. The reality is that there are a lot of people who would never step foot into a church if you invited them to attend; even if you told them they could receive a miraculous healing. Jesus didn't wait until he was in a Synagogue to heal the sick. He took care of it on the streets, in private homes, in the market place, and anywhere else he ended up. So don't be discouraged if you can't start your own supernatural healing ministry in the church tomorrow. Go do what Jesus told you to, and he will provide the increase he promised as well as many opportunities to partner with him. People will take notice of what is happening, and you will eventually be given even more opportunities as a result of your faithfulness.

Endnotes
1. Matthew 10:8
2. Mark 16:17-18
3. Acts 9:17-18
4. Matthew 11:11
5. 2 Corinthians 3:18
6. John 17:11
7. John 14:15
8. Matthew 13:15
9. Matthew 13:17
10. Matthew 13:23
11. Mark 16:17-18
12. Matthew 10:8

Going Deeper

1. Imagine a revolution in the church today. What do you think that would look like?

---

2. What are your thoughts on the mandates of Jesus discussed in this chapter? Are they really mandates? Or just suggestions?

---

3. Did anything in this chapter create a new level of passion with you to do more for Jesus?

---

4. Is there anything the believers in the New Testament did that you don't think is for today? Why, or why not?

Deeper Prayer

Jesus has given all of us a mandate, it's not a difficult one to obey, but it can be a little scary to take the first few steps. The great thing about taking steps of faith is that, God always honors it, and comes along side of us in our journey. He desires to do so much through us, and he longs for us to have the same desire. It's important to see him as a King, as well as a savior, and a friend. His role as King causes his mandate to carry a lot of weight, and as his followers, we have an obligation to carry out his orders. When we do, everything changes for the better. Here's a prayer you can pray to ask him for help in pursuing what he has for you:

Jesus, I long to do so much more for you. I long to see you move in my life in new, and exciting ways. And I long to see you work through me to impact the lives of others in ways that only you can do. Help me to be focused on your mission in the earth, and to be obedient to the directions, and guidance you gave to me in your word, as well as to the direction, and guidance from Holy Spirit. I recognize that obedience is not just about not sinning, it is also about following my King wherever you lead. Give me the strength to follow you, so that I can accomplish everything you have purposed for me to do.

CHAPTER EIGHT

ADDICTION

For anyone reading this book that's thinking about pursuing more of God, and pushing into a life of risk, I have a warning for you. This lifestyle is addictive. I haven't met anyone who was involved in a supernatural ministry who was able to walk away cold turkey, and forget about what they had experienced. Something happens when you see someone healed through your hands for the very first time. It gets you a little fired up, and all you want to do is go find more sick people, so that you can see more miracles. Every time I see a miracle I get excited. Even after witnessing thousands of supernatural healings, and making miracles a normal part of my lifestyle I still get excited about the fact that I have the awesome privilege of releasing God's love into people's lives. It's the greatest job that anyone could ever have. There is no greater high, and no greater honor than to be a part of what God is doing. I have already talked about the cost, but believe me when I tell you that every bit of it is entirely worth it. So before you step out that door, and start looking for sick people you need to understand that once you start, you won't be able to stop. You won't be able to turn it off, and do something else. You will be hooked for life. You'll end up sensitive to the promptings of Hoy Spirit everywhere you go, ready to freely give away what God has given to you. Canes, casts, and wheelchairs are all pretty obvious targets, and if you are willing to take the risk of engaging with those people, you will find yourself totally amazed by how quickly, and how often God shows up to work through you as you are obedient.

I keep a small wooden box on my desk that serves as a reminder of when this healing ministry went from powerless to powerful. In this box are a few pieces of paper, a prophecy I received when I was a teenager, and a few of the supernatural feathers I have found in different places. I'll tell you more about the feathers a little later. One piece of paper in the box has a few messages scribbled onto it that God had given to me on the day I first saw breakthrough in supernatural healing. They were words of knowledge about the conditions the Lord was going to heal through me on that day. I didn't know who they were for, or even when they would come into play, but I tucked that piece of paper into my pocket, and waited for the opportunity that God had already selected. That evening I shared those words of knowledge at a small gathering, and was excited to see three different people respond. The short version of the story is that God healed each one of them just as he had showed me he would. The other piece of paper in the box has the names of those who were healed that night, and what they were healed of. I keep the box close by for a couple of reasons. Every time I sit at my desk I am reminded of what was started on that first night, and all the other amazing miracles that have happened since. Abraham had a habit of building altars after pivotal moments in his life. I think they probably served as a reminder to him of what God had done at that time, or in that place. I'm sure he even reminisced whenever he walked past some of those altars during his journey's throughout Canaan. The box also reminds me that there is still a lot of sickness in the world that hasn't been ravaged by the kingdom of heaven. That's what drives me forward. I know what God can do, I have seen it firsthand time, and time again, and I know that when I pray people will be healed. So I keep going for it. I can't buy a box to store a note on every miracle I see, but these first few were pivotal that I keep them close. It reminds me when I first got addicted, and keeps me going for it when I run into sicknesses that don't disappear.

I chose the title of this chapter because I wanted to convey the message that it's ok to be an addict. Addiction typically carries a negative connotation to it because most people are addicted to things that hurt, or destroy their bodies, and lives. I've never been addicted to a drug, so I don't have a good personal barometer on how to compare being addicted to supernatural activity to a drug, or alcohol addiction. But I'll give it a shot because I think there is a similarity between the two. Addictions are uncontrollable. When a person gets addicted to a drug it quickly escalates to the point that they cannot function normally without it. It actually creates a new normality in their lives as everything begins to revolve around their drug of choice. Waiting for that next high consumes them throughout the day, and it's always on the forefront of their minds. When you minister with a power, and authority that supernaturally transforms lives in a matter of seconds, it becomes like a drug. It's addictive, and it grows to the point that it is almost uncontrollable. I was walking through the airport the other day thinking about how long it had been since I prayed with someone, or seen a miracle. It felt like it had been forever since the last time, so I was looking for people who stood out as needing prayer, probably similar to how an addict looks for a dealer. And then I remembered seeing a miracle about 18 hours earlier, and I started to laugh at myself because I realized how addicted to this I really am. I cannot get through a day without thinking about miracles. It's always on the forefront of my mind. It really is that addictive. I can't stop this thing, and I have no desire to ever give it up. I actually think God designed it that way. He knows how exhilarating it is to see someone's eyes open for the first time, and he knows that once you get a taste there is no turning back.

When I tell people about what God is doing through me they get excited because it's not what they consider to be normal. Supernatural stories are always interesting, even to the skeptics, because anything that happens outside the realm of what someone considers to be possible is exciting to hear about. Take the Bigfoot phenomenon for example; people are obsessed with the notion that this creature could exist to the point that they setup hidden cameras, and, organize stake outs to try to catch a glimpse of what no one has ever definitively documented. I can't imagine what these same people would do if an angel showed up on one of their videos. And then there's the amazing success of the Harry Potter books, and movies. These adventurous fantasy tales of a group of adolescent wizards have netted billions of dollars. Our society literally absorbs supernatural stories; people want to believe in the supernatural, and in a small way, it's like an addiction. They wait in long lines to see the latest movie on opening night, and think about it incessantly for weeks. Why? Because it is exciting to imagine the possibility of experiencing anything that is outside of what we perceive as normal. I like to tell other believers that I am not anyone special. God can do through anyone else what he does through me. This usually creates some of that same Harry Potter style excitement as they ponder the possibility that Jesus has already given them the authority to perform miracles. I took a short break from writing today to go meet up with someone who needed a miracle. She had an infection in her left eye that had persisted for several weeks, and it was starting to affect her eyesight. She was preparing to leave for a mission's trip a few days later, and her doctor had advised her not to travel in this condition, so she needed a miracle, and she needed it quickly. Well, of course, God showed up because that's what he does, and after a few short prayers the problem was gone. I always get excited when I see miracles, but I also like to see how people react. Some cry, some laugh, some dance, and some just stand there in complete shock. This young lady was shocked, and excited by what had just happened, but she was also getting excited about the possibility that she could be used in the same way. I shared with her, and her friends that this is what a normal Christian lifestyle should look like, and that idea seemed to resonate with, and excite them even more.

Each new miracle is like getting a fix. And each miracle makes me want to see other types of sicknesses healed. I'll see a knee healed, and that will make me want to go after someone whose leg is too short. Or I'll hear about someone who got up out of a wheelchair, and then I'll start searching for paraplegics. It's as if I am looking for a bigger miracle to satisfy my need to see God work supernaturally. It's actually kind of funny to think about it this way because comparing an addiction to the Christian lifestyle sounds a little silly. But I just can't get enough. David expressed it in a similar way in one of his Psalms[1] when he talked about his soul yearning, and his flesh crying out for God. He was pursuing God to the point that the passion turned into an addiction. Every part of his being would cry out to be in God's presence. David didn't get to experience God the way we do today, what he had was like a watered down version of what Jesus brought a few hundred years later. David cried out for everything he could have, and it's a great model for what we should be doing today; especially since we have access to so much more. I've spent a lot of hours on the floor crying out for more. Every time I come home after seeing a miracle I thank God for what he did, and then I immediately ask for an increase. "More Lord" is one of the most common prayer I pray because I know there is always more of him available, and no matter what he gives me I will keep crying out for more. The amazing thing is that he never ignores my request as long as I am actively releasing what he has already given. I spend what he gives me, and then he brings an increase to what I carry.

There is this concept within the healing ministry that sharing testimonies builds faith, and creates expectation, so we always like to share testimonies before praying for the sick. This tends to increase the faith of the people in attendance for the healing they need. One time, when Jesus visited his home town, he found a great lack of faith; Mark 6[2] records that "He could not do any miracles there, except lay his hands on a few sick people, and heal them. He was amazed at their lack of faith." I think this passage has a lot to do with honor as well, but let's stick with the faith piece for now. Even though I've seen people healed who had no faith, I still don't want to be in a room full of doubt; it tends to kill the atmosphere. What I really like is to walk into a room full of hunger, and expectation. Rev 19^3 says "the testimony of Jesus is the spirit of prophecy." Understanding what this verse means is incredibly powerful for anyone in ministry. One form of prophecy is a way to declare things into existence; prophecy has the power to change an event. If you prophesy to someone who is depressed, and call them happy, you are not simply telling them they are going to be happy in the future, you are actually declaring that into their life, and current situation. What we see in Revelation is that when we tell a story about what Jesus has already done it can cause a change in a present situation. That really changes the dynamic of testimonies. It changes it from being a simple story time that makes people happy about something God has done, into a prophetic moment where other people with the same condition can be healed. Read this carefully because it can make a huge difference in how you handle giving testimonies from this point forward. Sharing a testimony of what Jesus has done is a prophetic word that can bring a change to a current condition. Sharing a testimony about someone being healed of a cancerous tumor can cause a healing to immediately take place in someone's body that hears, or reads about the testimony. I shared earlier about the young lady whose left eye was healed, but there's another part I haven't told you yet. My wife's eyes had been bothering her for a few days; they were itchy, and irritated, probably from allergies. I sent her a text message that evening to share of this testimony, and she was instantly healed when she read the message. The testimony became prophetic. And this isn't limited to physical healings. Testimonies about anything Jesus has done can bring about the same results in others' lives that need a similar miracle. If he did it before, he will do it again! Keep that in mind the next time someone shares a testimony with you.

Here's another example; during one of the services on our New Zealand trip, the speaker invited anyone who had lost their sense of smell to come forward for healing. This was a condition he had recently seen a lot of healing in, so he shared a few testimonies, and then had anyone who needed that type of healing to come to the front. The way he did it was different than I had seen in the past; it was another learning experience for me. I had the privilege of being on the stage at that time with the rest of the ministry team, so I was able to see the expressions on the faces of everyone who came forward. The speaker didn't initially pray, instead he had someone bring him a few, oranges, and a bottle of perfume; he needed something with a strong scent, so he could test out their smelling ability. About 12, or 13 people lined up across the front of the stage, and all he did was take the, orange, and break it open just under their nose, then switched to the perfume when the, oranges ran out. The simple act of them coming forward when the testimony was given was enough for most of them to be healed. Smelling the, orange was the method he used to verify the healing had taken place. There were a few people who didn't get healed right away, and couldn't smell the, orange, so he quickly prayed for those, and I think all but one was completely healed. One lady had lost her sense of smell 40 years earlier, so you can imagine how thrilled she was to smell again. All of this from just sharing a story about what Jesus had previously done. This is the reason why I always instruct people after they receive a miracle to tell everyone they know what happened. This isn't to get me some kind of fame, it's to share what Jesus has done, so that more people will be healed. Imagine the response if someone who was healed of deafness shared the testimony before a deaf audience, and everyone's ears instantly opened! I heard someone say that testimony literally means "do it again." What Jesus has already done, he wants to do again!

Another exciting thing is that God loves to, orchestrate events that take us by surprise, and set someone up for a miracle. I was boarding a flight from Atlanta to San Antonio, and as I stepped onto the airplane I saw several people standing in the doorway with nowhere to sit. They had boarding passes, and assigned seat numbers, but the row numbers they were assigned didn't exist on the airplane. Apparently the airplanes were swapped out, and the configuration of seats on this flight was different than originally planned. They each had a legitimate boarding pass, but no one caught the mistake until after they made it onto the aircraft. We were all eventually kicked off the airplane, so that the staff could sort out the seat assignments, and when I re-boarded I found out the man sitting next to me had Alzheimer's disease. He wouldn't have been sitting anywhere near me if the seats hadn't been jumbled up, so I knew this was a setup. His wife made a comment about flight safety, and then made the sign of the cross before we left, so I knew she believed in God. That always makes it a little easier because you don't know if the guy you're about to pray for is an atheist that might get angry when you talk about Jesus. The last thing I want to do is sit on a two hour flight next to someone who is mad at me. After the flight took off, and we leveled out at cruising altitude, I leaned over to the couple next to me to share a story with them, and offer prayer. I told them it wasn't an accident that we were seated next to each other, and that God had a plan for their lives that included a supernatural healing. They happily received prayer after I shared about the miracles I had seen, and I really enjoyed declaring healing into this man's mind. I had never prayed for anyone with Alzheimer's prior to this, but that didn't mean anything to me. I've seen God heal lots of other stuff, so the type of sickness I encounter is irrelevant. I actually like encountering new sicknesses because I want to see everything healed. I don't know what happened that day, and I haven't seen either of them since, but I do know they encountered God's love, and that's enough for me to get excited. I know that something happens every time I pray. I know this because in Mark 11[4] Jesus said that if we believe what we ask for it will be given to us. So even if I don't see an immediate result I can still walk away believing a miracle took place; anything less is a lack of faith.

Miracles, that's what Jesus is all about. The miracle of salvation, the miracle of healing; everything he does is creative, and miraculous. And when people see miracles they no longer have an argument for the existence of God. When an atheist encounters the healing power of God it really messes up their belief system. Think about that for a minute. Think about how impactful a miracle can be to someone. The physical miracle will, of course, have a major impact, but think about what's going on in their head when it happens. When non-Christians get healed, especially the ones who completely deny the existence of God, it flips their perception of theology upside down. I don't always ask about salvation when I'm ministering healing on the streets because, often times, I think they know in the instant they are touched, what they need to do. If someone walked up to you on the street, and gave you a million dollars you would be incredibly thankful, and you would probably ask them what they wanted you to do in return. Jesus doesn't require anything in return for his love, but the reaction to miracles is similar because it's normal to feel indebted to someone who helps you out of a major problem. You can't forget about the day a cancerous tumor disappeared from your body; you think about that for the rest of your life. You can't not be affected when you encounter God. When Moses walked up to the burning bush, it changed him for life. When Jesus knocked Saul off of his horse, it rocked his world. The same God that was involved in both of those encounters is the one people encounter when miracles occur in their life. I was thinking about some of the major world religions that exist today, and how Christianity is the only one I know of where miracles occur. I have never heard of a Muslim Cleric going into a hospital to heal the sick. Nor have I heard of a Hindu Guru taking to the streets of India to perform miracles. Jesus stands apart from every other belief system in so many ways, but the miracles are the ones that stand out so clearly to non-believers, and it's easy for anyone to get excited when they see something humanly impossible occur in front of their eyes.

Jesus has healed someone of every disease known to man, so

taking those testimonies to groups of people who need the same miracle can be the catalyst for a major transformation in your city. There's no reason why he won't work in, and through you to heal the lives of the people you encounter every day. I love the model Jesus portrayed for us. Walking from city to city, stopping to teach the crowds about the principles of his kingdom. He wasn't just re-teaching what the religious leaders had to say. He was breathing life back into a belief system that had become dusty, and riddled with leaders who were more concerned with themselves than the people they supposedly served. People don't want to follow a belief system that is powerless to help them, and that's exactly the situation they were in when Jesus showed up. Add to this that he performed miracles everywhere he went. The scriptures tell us he drew large crowds on a regular basis. Can you imagine 5,000 people following some guy through town everywhere he goes? It sounds to me like they were infatuated with what Jesus had to say, and what he was doing. Of course, this was different from many of the street preachers we see today who stand on street corners with megaphones screaming at everyone that they are going to burn in hell. No one responds to that type of "ministry." If anything, it turns people away because they start to think all of God's followers are angry people bent on the destruction of humanity in hell. But if you stood on the street corner, and healed people, well that's a different story all together. And if you do it long enough, people will start lining up when they see you coming. People were addicted to what Jesus had because it was good. They chased him down dirt roads to get a small taste of what he had to offer, and he never disappointed them.

    I hope this chapter did two things for you. I hope it got you a little excited about the possibility of what God can, and will do, through you, if you are willing to take him at his word. And I hope that the excitement will turn to addiction once you start stepping out. I use the addictive term loosely, but I really do mean it when I say that it's a hard lifestyle to get away from once you start. Maybe it's better to compare it with adrenaline junkies who get thrills from sky diving, or racing cars around a track. Those can be exhilarating events, but they don't even come close to seeing bones grow, or diseases disappear. I really don't understand why more people don't push into this type of lifestyle. I suppose it's easy to sit back, and let someone else take the risk, but when the payoff is as amazing as what I see every week, I'm a little shocked that more people aren't lining up to get involved.

You can't not be affected when you encounter God.

One of the focuses of our ministry is to spend time each week with some of the impoverished residents of Washington D.C. The Lord led us to a spot in the poorest part of the city where, on any given day, there are 30-40 people sitting in the parking lot of a laundromat. Many of them are struggling with addictions, or homeless, or both. We have met veterans who were dishonorably discharged, and can't get work as a result. We have met ex-offenders who no one will hire because of their past. So they sit in a parking lot, because they feel like they have nothing better to do. They are, quite literally, at rock bottom. I can honestly say that ministering in this parking lot is one of our favorite things to do. Sometimes we pray for healing. Sometimes we pray for employment. Sometimes we pray for freedom from addiction. And God shows up every time. We have seen hundreds of people healed, and some of them were drunk, or high when it happened! That will really mess up your theology. We have had reports of people getting jobs a week after we prophesied it into their lives. We have even had people walk up, and start confessing their sins without any prompting, or questions from us. And every week, many of the regulars come to us as if we are extended members of their family. We spend time with them to share God's love, and see their lives fully transformed.

I carry what other people need, and if I hold onto it, I am no better than the guy in Matthew 25[5] who buried the talent in the ground. I have to give away everything he has given to me. Back in the 1980's, a musician named Carman put out a song titled "Addicted to Jesus." It never gained any popularity in the mainstream, but the lyrics were really powerful. There are so many things we can waste our time, and energy on, but wouldn't it be better if we focused on something that was actually important? There are so many things we could be addicted to, but wouldn't it be great if we were all addicted to helping others? If you want to see the world change, the solution is really simple; go get addicted to a miracle lifestyle. You're going to love the results!

Endnotes
1. Psalm 84:2
2. Mark 6:5-6
3. Revelation 19:10
4. Mark 11:24
5. Matthew 25:25

Going Deeper

1. What do you think about this idea of being addicted to the work of Jesus?

----

2. Have you ever seen a miracle happen when you prayed for someone? If so, how did it make you feel? How did the person respond?

----

3. Is it better to be addicted to the idea of miracles, or to be addicted to loving the person in front of you?

----

4. On a scale of 1 to 10, How excited are you about being used by God?

Deeper Prayer

I know, thinking about a miraculous lifestyle from the perspective of addiction is a little strange. But I want you to realize that representing Jesus does have a similar effect on our lives. There is something about being in his presence that leaves us wanting more. There is something about being his hands and feet that make us want to be used even more. It's exhilarating, and it is for everyone. Here's a great prayer to pray, if you want to experience this type of lifestyle:

Jesus, I want to be addicted to you above everything else. I want to live a life that is constantly searching for new ways I can be with you, new experiences I can have with you, and new ways I can represent you to others. Increase my faith to have a greater expectation to be used by you in any situation I encounter. And let every new encounter bring with it an increase to do even more for you. I want to see the world changed. I want the world to experience your love, and I want to want these things even more. Increase my desire for you, and help me to be a walking encounter for others.

CHAPTER NINE

PRESENCE

Spending time in God's presence is easily the most enjoyable, and rewarding experience in the universe. I'm not talking about traditional prayer where you go to God with a list of problems that need to be fixed. I'm also not talking about random conversations you have with God throughout your day. Both of those are part of your relationship, and there is a time for each, but right now I am talking about just hanging out with God like you would your best friend. I love to sit on my couch, invite the presence of the Holy Spirit, and then just soak. I imagine that I am a sponge soaking up all of God's goodness. It's a great place to be. No, it's the best place to be. God enjoys spending time with us, and these quality moments of resting in his presence are how we get recharged, and renewed for ministry. A relationship has to be so much more than just asking for stuff all the time. God has everything we need, and he wants to have those types of discussions with us as well, but we can't be so focused on what we want that it becomes a one sided relationship. Sometimes it's good to just soak in his presence, and listen to what he has to say. One of the Psalms[1] says "In Your presence is fullness of joy." It says fullness of joy, not a small dose of joy, not just enough joy to get you through the workday, but fullness of joy. I sometimes find myself laughing during these moments. The fullness of his joy makes me so happy that I cannot contain it, and it comes out in uncontrollable bursts of laughter that cannot be contained. It's also in these moments that we learn to listen to his voice, and learn to discern what he is saying.

God is speaking more often than we are listening. I am confident that God is always speaking to us, but we are so easily distracted that we miss out on what he has to say. Our lives get incredibly busy with work, kids, maintaining the house, and a slew of other routine tasks that we rarely make time for ourselves to just rest, let alone to rest with him. When you learn to slow down, and listen, you will find that God loves to share his secrets with those who take spending quality time with him seriously. If I have learned anything in my journey with God it is this; the more time that you intentionally set aside to be in his presence, the more he will show up, and show off through you. One of the great misunderstandings of Christianity is that we think we can spend just a few minutes each day, or maybe even each week, with God, and then expect him to show up, and do a miracle when we run into a problem. God loves doing miracles, they are never based on our merits, but there is something to be said for seriously contending for more of him. Daniel is someone who really knew the importance of pressing into God's presence. We see phrases throughout his book like "Three times a day he got down on his knees, and prayed[2]," or "I turned to the Lord God, and pleaded with him in prayer, and petition[3]" that give us a glimpse into his prayer habits. At one point Gabriel was dispatched to provide Daniel with the answer he needed, but it took 21 days for Gabriel to break through the demonic forces that were slowing him down[4]. I doubt Daniel prayed for five minutes, and then gave up. I suspect he kept praying during that 21 day window until the answer arrived.

If you want to be someone that God powerfully moves through, you will need to understand the importance of his presence. God's presence isn't something we just enter into when we go to church. For some that might be the case, but the goal should be to get into his presence whenever, and wherever you can. I have actually gotten to the point in my life where I am not happy if I'm not in his presence. I'd trade an hour of TV for an hour with God any day. Because I have come to realize that the more time you spend in his presence the more of his presence soaks into your life. Imagine your spirit is a giant sponge, and when you are out of God's presence for a while you get all dried out. If you wanted to soak a physical sponge you would put it under a water faucet. Your spiritual sponge is the same way, except the water faucet is God's presence. I don't want to get dried out, so I purposefully find ways to get into his presence throughout the day to soak up his goodness. I don't approach these sessions as a time of devotion to read the Bible, or to ask for a laundry list of items. This soaking time is a chance to just sit, and listen. As if you were sitting on the carpet in front of the Father's throne, listening to everything he has to say. There are certain people that make you feel good just when you are around them. They have the type of personality that makes you happy to be with them, and it creates a desire to be with them, and around them even more. That's what these soaking times are about. To spend quality time with someone who literally creates something new in your life every time he speaks.

Let's put this into practice. I want you to try an experiment. Set aside some time each day to simply rest in his presence. I recommend that you initially start with 15 minutes, but if you stick with it you will find that 15 minutes isn't enough. It will quickly increase to 30 minutes, an hour, and even longer. And eventually you'll want to steal away for a few minutes throughout the day to re-plug into him. During these times try not to speak. Just listen. Find some soft worship music to play in the background, get a comfortable place to sit, and then invite his presence. This might be a little tough at first, if you're not used to just quietly sitting for long periods of time. But don't give up too soon; push into this for at least a few weeks, and I promise you will begin to feel a shift in the atmosphere around you. One of the best ways I have found to get started in these soaking sessions is to invite God's presence by simply saying something like "come Holy Spirit." That's not some secret mantra, or formula that guarantees success; it's just a simple phrase that's easy to remember, and quite honestly, I think God likes short prayers. I know I especially like short prayers when food is involved. Seriously, God really loves to spend time with us, and when we invite his presence he is quick to show up. He wants to be with you more than you want to be with him, so there isn't any convincing you need to do, just invite him, and he will show up. Practice this experiment for a few weeks, and you will begin to have encounters with God like you never have had before.

There's another thing I like to do in addition to soaking that keeps me in God's presence all day long. I heard someone make a suggestion once about wearing a timer that would set off an alarm at certain intervals throughout the day. They would use this timer as a reminder to pause for a quick minute of worship time. This particularly person had hers set for every ten minutes. Every ten minutes throughout her day she would hear the beeping, or feel the vibrating, and be reminded to worship God. Every ten minutes she would take just a few seconds to tell God how awesome he is, thank him for his goodness, or whatever other praises came to mind. Then she would go back to whatever was happening before the alarm went off again. There are a couple things I find amazing about this routine. First, it's hard to be affected by the world around you when you are praising God every ten minutes. The normal routines of the day don't drain you as much when you're focused on the King. And the distractions that normally get you upset don't bend you out of shape. Second, God inhabits the praises of his people, so if you are in a constant state of praise, the presence of God will constantly be with you. His presence will always be hovering over you. That's my favorite part because that's what I always want. When I first started using one of these timers, I thought it would be a distraction to get interrupted every ten minutes, but it actually turned out to be the perfect short break. Five seconds of praise every ten minutes keeps you focused on what really matters. The funny thing is that I even started anticipating when the timer would go off because I was ready to get after some more praise. I would pull the timer off of my belt to see how much time was left because I was excited about getting back in the presence. I was still on active duty with the military when I first started this, and when you work in an environment like the Pentagon, it's good to shift the atmosphere as often as possible. And you know what? God would show up at my desk. His presence would descend in a powerful way, and change the atmosphere in the office. Today, I use my Fitbit for this same purpose, though it is limited to how many alarms I can set throughout the day. These two experiments together are a powerhouse combination that will bring you closer to God than you have ever been before. Give it a shot, and find out for yourself.

The fifteenth chapter of John is one of my favorite sections of the entire Bible. I love it because it tells us the story of Jesus having a very candid conversation with the disciples about the relationship they were to have with him from that point forward. Jesus had a lot of candid conversations with his disciples, but this one took on a little different tone. It has more of a heart to heart feel as he used, yet another parable, to explain how to stay plugged into him. This time, he used a grapevine to create an analogy of what our relationship with him should look like. Just like a tree gets its nutrients through the trunk, and then into the branches, a grapevine functions in the same manner. The vines are like the trunk of a tree; there not quite as large, but they are the connection point for all the branches. And those branches cannot exist apart from the vine. If you were to cut the branch off of a grapevine, or any other type of plant, it would instantly begin to die because it would no longer have a connection point to receive nutrients. The branch is also where the buds form that grow into the shoots that hold the sweet, and edible fruit. Grapevines that receive very little water, or even bad water will not yield as high quality grapes as those that receive a fresh supply of clean water on a regular basis. It is in these few verses that Jesus gives us the key to how to live a supernatural lifestyle. He shows that it is all connected to relationship, and that we cannot be fruitful, or even survive, without remaining connected to him, because when that connection is severed the spiritual nutrients we need to flourish will be cut off. It has to be a continually abiding connection that focuses on being in his presence that keeps us from withering. Most Christians really struggle in this area because it is difficult in today's society to start, and maintain a routine that encourages spiritual growth. Many believers are barely hanging onto the branch by just a few strands; enough to stay alive, but not enough to operate from a position of power, and authority. Remaining in him is more than just a passive barely connected state.

Remain in me, as I also remain in you[5]

Jesus makes it clear that remaining in him is the key to receiving from the Father. This cannot be passive, it has to be an active approach that is constantly seeking to stay connected; just like a baby who receives nourishment from its mother, the milk does not automatically flow, the baby must actively pull the milk out. So when we become Christians, we really need to learn right away that our daily routine needs to include more than just a cursory ten minutes of prayer on the way to work to put a check in the prayer box for the day. And it can't be limited to only reading the verse of the day on some website without digging deeper into the treasure of his word. The word "remain" in this context means to stay in the place that one has been occupying. Notice it doesn't mean to go back, and forth, or to occupy only when necessary for defense. It is a continual location of existence where we permanently setup camp, and stay. I also think that this is a reciprocal process. We have to remain in him in, order for him to remain in us. I'll even take that a little further, and say that I think it is automatically reciprocal. We don't have to wonder if our soaking sessions are enough to keep him interested in us. We don't have to worry about whether, or not he is remaining in us. We can live knowing that anytime we connect to God he will automatically be connected to us. We can know that staying connected to him keeps him connected to us. This is what he wants. He wants to have a continuous connection; we should all be like conduits connected to him, so that his power can flow through us, and into others. But most believers don't stay connected. It's a place we run back to when we are in trouble, or when we need something, but it's not always a place where we dwell on a daily regular basis. I think this is mostly a result of not practicing being in his presence often enough. I love to play chess, but one thing I learned is that you can't be a good chess player if you never practice. You need to play the game every day, and when you aren't playing you should be studying strategy to learn different techniques. Playing once a month will never make you an expert. Staying connected to God is very similar. We need to have such an insatiable hunger for God that we spend hours with him every day. It should be the automatic default position when we wake up, and when we go to sleep. Because it is in this place of connection that God is able to work through us in mighty ways that bring him more glory.

This is to my Father's glory, that you bear much fruit[6]

God wants you to bear fruit because it brings him glory. And not just a little bit of fruit either; it's much fruit! Matthew 7[7] says "You will know them by their fruits." Do you know any Christians that aren't producing any fruit? If you do, they must not be focused on staying connected to the vine. Do you know any Christians whose fruit is bitter? They are probably trying to feed their spirit from the things of the world instead of the things of God. God wants to be glorified through the fruit that we bear, but if we aren't staying plugged into him, how can we possibly receive what we need? The truth is that we can't. God can use anyone in any way he likes. He can drop his anointing on those who are seeking, and those who are not. He can choose those who fast, and those who do not. But a consistent life of supernatural activity is often born from a desire to stay connected, and it certainly cannot survive without that connection. When I started on this journey I spent a lot of time specifically focused on how to stay connected because I realized that this was an important element of living the type of lifestyle God called all of us to pursue. I wanted, and still want to see him glorified more, and more each day. I'll see a few people healed, and a few others not healed, and I quickly find myself seeking more of his presence, so that he can receive more glory when more people are miraculously healed. What's great about this is that God wants you to be successful in the work he has called you to do, because the more successful you are, the more glory he receives. People cannot be unaffected when they see miracles. I see people who don't believe in Jesus get healed on the streets, and you can tell by the look on their faces that they really don't understand what just happened, except that it didn't seem normal. They recognize in some way that they had an encounter with Jesus, and they don't always know how to respond except to say thank you. That thank you gives more glory to God, and every time that person thinks about what happened they will be reminded of God's love, and even in the quietness of their thoughts, God will receive more glory. It's what he deserves, and it should be every Christian's goal to go out, and get more for him.

My father is the gardener[8]

My wife and I used to have a fairly large garden that we grew vegetables, and fruits in every year. We learned a lot about how to get the right amount of water onto the plants, when to prune, and how to recognize when it was time to harvest. It seemed inevitable that a few plants would fail to produce fruit each year, and others would completely die, or never really get a good start, because they didn't absorb all the necessary nutrients needed for survival. I wish I could have just dug a hole, dropped in a plant, and stepped back to watch it grow, but as the gardener, I had a responsibility to maintain everything in the garden. The plants didn't choose where they got planted, or how often they receive water. They only do what they were created to do, and when they receive the proper balance of nutrients they flourish, and produce great crops. Tomato plants produce tomatoes; they don't produce anything else, no matter how perfect the conditions seem. We see in this same chapter that the Father is the gardener in this parable. He is a gardener that provides the exact perfect blend of nutrients that we need to be fruit bearers in his kingdom. We have this guarantee that as long as we remain in Jesus all the nutrients we need to flourish, and produce fruit will automatically be available to us. And we also see that the Father will prune back the branches that bear fruit in, order to make them even more fruitful. This spiritual pruning takes on a lot of different meaning across the spectrum of churches, and belief systems. Some think that anytime they encounter a problem, it is God doing a little pruning, and that they just have to endure the pain until it passes. That's not always the case. God's pruning process is to eliminate the superfluous branches of our life that restrict us from having an even deeper relationship with him. But he doesn't make us sick. He doesn't inject a disease into the vine. Whoever came up with the notion that God makes us sick to teach us different lessons didn't have a full grasp of who God is. Good fathers don't give bad gifts to their kids, but they do create environments for their kids to flourish. Pruning removes something to make the rest of the plant more productive. He will often prune back issues like pride, anger, jealousy, and other faults that tend to crop up like weeds in our lives. Each issue he cuts away may result in a twinge of pain; another way to say this is that he disciplines those that he loves[9], and discipline is rarely enjoyable. We should always welcome these pruning sessions because they make us better equipped to represent him, and bring him more glory as a result.

Apart from me you can do nothing[10]

This is such a key element to serving God. Without God, you cannot do anything! When I pray for the sick, I know miracles are possible only because of Jesus. When I command demons to leave, I know they have to obey because of Jesus. And when I release peace, and joy into someone's life, I know it will happen because Jesus has already made it possible. But all of this is only possible if we remain in him. So if we cannot do anything without him, what does it mean when our prayers fail to bring results? So many Christians don't see the supernatural power of God at work in their lives, or churches because they are not staying plugged in. It's just that simple. We have allowed the routines of our lives to take up our time, and attention to the point that it is actually hurting the world. I'm confident that if every Christian was truly representing Jesus we wouldn't have any crime, or any disease, or any of the other problems that plague the planet. This isn't a slam on churches; it's a call to action. We have failed this world by not properly representing Jesus to every walk of society. And the Church cannot depend on a handful of preachers to stay plugged in while everyone else stays comfortable. There are churches, and ministers that see thousands of miracles every month, and then there are churches that don't see anything. That's a pretty wide gap to close; to go from one end of the spectrum to the other is a big leap, but it can be done with the simple step of remaining in him. Making remaining in him a normal part of life puts you in a position to soak up his presence throughout the day, and release it whenever you come across someone in need.

Now remain in my love[11]

1 John 4[12] says that "God is love." That's what soaking in the presence is really all about; enjoying God's love by sitting at his feet, and spending time with him. The way I see it is that we have an obligation to love the world. But how can we love the world if we are not full of his love? The truth is that human love doesn't go far enough. There are some people I cannot love on my own. Not because I want to hate them, but because my human nature drives me to despise people who hurt others. But when I soak in his presence, I'm refilled with his love, and it changes the dynamic of how I see the world. I often ask God to let me see the world through his eyes, so that when I walk down the street every person I see will be viewed from the

perspective of a loving God who wants to have a relationship with them, and change their lives for the better. But I don't think we can make this request flippantly, or as part of a 15 minute weekly prayer plan. Remaining in his love, and being loved by him are two different things. God loves everyone, but Jesus said we can only remain in his love if we keep his commands[13]. Being in his love puts you in the friendship category, and gives you access to the supernatural gifts that he has available for anyone who is willing to take the time to soak in his presence.

Being in his presence is the best location anyone could ever spend their time. Remaining in his presence 24/7 guarantees a life of miracles. This is the place where we can clearly hear his voice, and receive the guidance, and wisdom we need to get through the day. God's supernatural ability is not limited to healing the sick, or raising the dead. He can do the "smaller" stuff too. He can improve your relationships, and shift the atmosphere in your workplace just as easily as placing a new lung in someone's body. And it all starts by pursuing in him in the simplest of ways; resting. I cannot get through a day without stopping to rest in his presence along the way. It's the first thing I do when I wake up, and throughout my day I stop, and soak every chance I get. I intentionally make time for these moments because they are more important to me than anything else. I cannot get enough of his presence, and I will never be satisfied with what I have already received, because I know that there is always more. There is no greater honor than to carry his presence with me everywhere I go. And every day I pray the same prayer. More Lord!

Endnotes
1. Psalm 16:11 (NASB)
2. Daniel 6:10
3. Daniel 9:3
4. Daniel 10:13
5. John 15:4

6. John 15:8
7. Matthew 7:16
8. John 15:1
9. Hebrews 12:6
10. John 15:5
11. John 15:9
12. 1 John 4:8
13. John 15:10

Going Deeper

1. How much time do you spend in God's presence right now?

---

2. Do you think you need to spend more time in his presence? Can you physically do it?

---

3. Are you ready to take your relationship with God to a deeper level?

---

4. Is there anything that scares you about spending time in God's presence?

Deeper Prayer

Soaking in God's presence may be a new idea to you, I know it was new to me when I first heard about it. It was a little awkward to just sit there on the couch, and wait for God to show up. But over time, it has become such a normal process for me that keeps my relationship with God exciting. Since this is a relationship, we need to be intentional about spending more time with the one we love. Are you ready to go deeper? Pray this prayer, then wait a few minutes, and listen for his voice:

Jesus, I need more of you! I need more of you in my family life, in my relationships, in my work life, and in every other part of my life. I need more of your presence. Help me to plug into you every day, and to stay connected to the vine, so that your presence can flow through me, and change the situations around me. I want to be your hands and feet to a hurting world, and I realize that pursuing a deeper relationship with you is the key to seeing the world changed. Come Holy Spirit. Fill this space. I want to spend time with you.

CHAPTER TEN

ANGELS

The role of the angelic in a Christian's life is always an interesting subject to tackle because it can sometimes get a little strange when we discuss supernatural beings. This is true when demonic possession is discussed as well, and I think the reason people are a little weirded out by it is because the movie industry has created a lot of films over the years that cover supernatural subjects from a disturbing perspective. Most of society is actually very interested in the supernatural because of these movies. Just look at the revenues brought in from the stories about vampires, paranormal activity, and child sorcery for proof. The society of the world is paying millions of dollars every year to be entertained by supernatural stories, and yet the church is avoiding the discussion. So I want to set the record straight right up front that it is ok to have these types of discussions because angels are part of God's creation, and they have a role to play in his plan just as each one of us have a role to play. Angels are given assignments that have brought followers of God into encounters with angelic beings since the earliest days of creation, and those encounters continue even today. The first mention of an angel in the Bible occurs just after Adam, and Eve were kicked out the garden. This angel was sent to guard the entrance, so that no one could gain access to the tree of life[1]. Later we see angels having conversations with Abraham before they head off to destroy Sodom, and Gomorrah[2]. Weaved throughout the pages of scripture we see that some came to strengthen, some were sent to deliver revelation, others delivered warnings, and all of them accomplished exactly what God sent them to do.

In the beginning of Exodus 33[3] God offered to send an angel to lead the Israelites into the Promised Land, and later in the chapter we see that Moses refused by telling God that he didn't want an angel, he wanted Him. It was an interesting dialogue, and I think Moses got it right. God was offering an angel in his place because the Israelites had angered him to the point that if he continued to hang around he would probably start killing them off. Moses was pretty quick to respond that if God wasn't leading them into the Promised Land he didn't want to go either. His desire was to be with God not angels. I think in this instance God was actually testing Moses to see if he had the hunger to ask for more, and I think in this case Moses got it right. But that story had colored my thinking for a long time to believe that I didn't need angels because I had the Holy Spirit, and I had Jesus, and I didn't want to trade that access for anyone, or anything else. I thought that if I started asking for angels to help in my ministry, I might be accepting a trade instead of pursuing more of God. I thought the role of the angelic was more in the realm of overseeing the bigger picture of God's plans, and only interacting with humans when it was necessary for them to fulfill that role. But I have come to realize that it's not an either, or situation for us. We can get all of God, and angelic assistance together. They are partnering with God as we are, so we should learn to ask God to send his angels to assist us in our missions. There are many verses that show us a glimpse into the interaction between angels, and humans.

What grabbed my attention the most was the events that happened immediately after the temptation of Jesus. In Matthew 4[4] it says "Then the devil left him, and angels came, and attended him." He was hungry, and fresh off of a victorious argument with Satan when some angels showed up to strengthen him. Later in the garden of Gethsemane we see a similar situation take place. Luke 22[5] tells us that "An angel from heaven appeared to him, and strengthened him." Wait a minute. Angels showed up to help Jesus? If the creator of the universe was strengthened by angels while he was in human form, I think the rest of us could use their help as well. The author of Hebrews poses a question that allows us to peer into the overarching role of the angelic. "Are not all angels ministering spirits sent to serve those who will inherit salvation?[6]" Angels exist to help us. Their mission is to help us accomplish ours, and their capabilities far exceed what is humanly possible. Having the angelic show up to help with anything we do seriously increases the odds of success. Anytime they showed up in scripture they did so with great power, and authority. Elisha knew they were present in 2 Kings[7], "the mountain was full of horses, and chariots of fire all around Elisha," so he wasn't afraid of the human army encroaching on his position. John started to bow down to the angel describing the events to him in Revelation 22[8], but the angel quickly stopped him, and reintroduced himself as a fellow servant. "I am a fellow servant with you, and with your fellow prophets, and with all who keep the words of this scroll." And Peter was busted out of jail when an angel showed up to open the door in Acts 12[9].

It's easy to wonder why God created the angels because he really doesn't need them. He really doesn't need us either. God could speak anything into, or out of existence a lot quicker than waiting for an angel, or human to act on his commands. He created the universe with just a few words, and created us with just a few more words, so why would he want to use an intermediary to accomplish anything? I don't think we'll ever figure out the exact answer to that question on this side of eternity, but we can infer a few reasons why. If God didn't use us to accomplish his will, then it would almost be a waste of his time creating us in the first place. And I think the same could be said for the angelic. I for one don't want to waste God's time, so I'm constantly looking for another opportunity to release his love. I can't sit still when

I see someone who needs a touch from God because I know he wants to heal everyone. And I know that there are angels waiting to release healing, so I don't want their assignments to be cancelled. I think they get just as excited about seeing miracles as we do, and I want them involved in every aspect of ministry I push into. I also think that if you are not doing what God has designed you for, there is likely an angel who can't do their job. Think about that for a minute. Angels could be waiting for you to step into your role, so that they can start doing what they were created for. I sure hope I'm not keeping any angels on the bench.

We see angels with different assignments in the Bible, but the stories that interest me the most are the ones where they have a prolonged interaction with the person God has sent them to. I think about Johns visions of the end times, and how the angelic were used to guide him, and explain to him what was happening[10]. Gabriel showing up to tell Mary she was pregnant[11] is pretty awesome, but spending a long time, or even several long sessions with an angel has got to be even more exciting. I love the interaction between John, and his heavenly guides as each new scene unfolds, and each new mystery keeps him baffled by what is happening. They describe in great detail what was happening, and in some cases John was even instructed not to write down what he heard spoken aloud. He was given a glimpse of what must transpire at some point, but not all of it was allowed to be shared. At one point John asked one of the angels for a scroll he was holding[12]. I wonder if he was planning to unroll it, and read its contents, or to tuck it away for a little light reading later on; regardless of his plans, the angel instructed him to eat the scroll. Daniel had similar experiences where angels were sent to show him futuristic events[13], and I think what we see in these accounts is that God wants to share what he is doing with all of us, and he often uses the angelic to deliver the message. I've read, and heard about countless stories of angelic encounters happening in our time, and it always excites me to know that God is still working in supernatural ways that often challenge us to trade in some of our critical thinking for a little childlike faith.

In Genesis 28[14], Jacob had a dream where he saw the heavens opened, and angels using a stairway to ascend into, and descend from heaven. Angels were moving between the two realms, and the open heaven is what allowed them to do this. If we jump over to the last verse in John chapter one we see Jesus use a very similar statement when he describes to Nathaniel that he will "see heaven open, and the angels of God ascending, and descending on the Son of Man.[15]" The open heaven was the avenue by which the angels were ascending, and descending in Jacob's dream, and that same avenue would be used for Jesus as well. So the key point that stands out here is that living under an open heaven will almost guarantee the operation of angels in your life. So then the question that naturally follows is "how do we live under an open heaven?" I'm glad you asked. Some people believe that when Jesus died on the cross an open heaven was established for all believers. We don't see this specifically in scripture, but we do see heaven open when Jesus was baptized[16], and throughout the New Testament we see angels interacting with the disciples in a variety of new ways. Another way to think about it is that any believer can pursue an open heaven. Jesus said in John 14[17] that we would do even greater things than him; I'm not sure that could that be possible unless we operate under the same open heaven as he did.

Psalm 104, and Hebrews 1[18] say he "makes his angels winds, and his ministers a flame of fire." This verse by itself doesn't help much in this discussion, but when you read it in conjunction with the account of what happened to the disciples in the upper room in Acts 2[19] it adds an interesting element to the story. "Suddenly a sound like the blowing of a violent wind came from heaven, and filled the whole house where they were sitting. They saw what seemed to be tongues of fire that separated, and came to rest on each of them." Of course we know this as the moment when the Holy Spirit being given to the disciples, but it's interesting that there was wind, and there was fire, both of which are used to describe angels in the previous two verses. Then we see John the Baptist saying in Luke 3[20] that Jesus would "baptize you with the Holy Spirit, and fire." The fire was described separately from the Holy Spirit. Angels are often described in the scripture as being in close proximity to God, whether it is around the throne, riding on horses with Jesus, or visiting with Abraham, we see angels working side by side with God. So it stands to reason that the wind mentioned in Acts 2 was possibly a host of angels coming into the room along with the Holy Spirit. I recently heard someone say that kings never travel by themselves. They always travel with an entourage. So it makes sense that wherever the Holy Spirit goes, there will always be angels in tow.

    I was praying in my living room one morning, and as I moved about the room I felt my hand bump into something. I looked around real quick thinking maybe I bumped a piece of furniture, but there wasn't anything close enough for me to touch. There also wasn't anyone else in the room, so I could only assume I bumped into something I couldn't see. Later that same day I heard footsteps in my bedroom when I woke up from a nap even though I was the only one home. These types of events began occurring around the same time I started asking God to send angels to assist me. I actually started by asking for my eyes to be opened to the spiritual realm because I had sensed that angels had been showing up from time to time, and I wanted to be more in tune to what was happening around me; especially in my own home. But I wasn't sure how to pray because praying for angelic help, or even the ability to see them was still a gray area in my thinking. So I found myself trying to justify my prayers to God because I wanted to make sure that God knew I wasn't trying to pursue angels over him. But as I developed a better understanding of the role of the angelic I approached my requests a little differently. I had actually hoped that an angel would show up right away, and start conversing with me like they did with Daniel, or John, but it didn't happen that way. It started with hearing, and feeling these supernatural beings in my home, and occasionally feeling them walk past me in church services. I then began to ask God to send the angelic for specific purposes like healing the sick, or commissioning other believers for their purposes, or to just come, and release his presence.

There's another time that I was in my living room praying a few months after this invisible angelic encounter when I noticed a small white feather suspended four feet off the ground on the other side of the room. I had heard of feathers supernaturally appearing in some church services, but this was the first time I had ever seen anything like this. I decided to go grab hold of this feather, so I could take a closer look. I walked to the other side of the room, and as I got close the feather shot up into the air another foot, and also moved a few more feet in front of me at the same time. If the suspended feather in midair initially caught my curiosity, the feather moving away from me definitely had my full attention. I still wanted to grab hold of it even though it moved away from me, and I didn't even give it a second thought. I took another step forward, and reached out my hand, palm up, in the hope that it would float down into my hand, or that I could sneak up from underneath it. Sneaking up on supernatural feathers, yeah that sounds a little strange. Well I was partially successful in my sneak attack, and managed to get the feather into the palm of my hand, but in the same split second that it touched my hand it shot up again, and then disappeared. Now I don't know if this was a feather that God decided to create, and float in my house, or if a feather fell from an angel's wing, but what I do know is that God was doing something to catch my attention. And I wouldn't be surprised if an angel was in the room holding onto the other end of that feather.

A few months after this feather incident we were in New Zealand, as I mentioned in an earlier chapter, and during one of the post service prayer sessions a feather appeared in midair, and fell onto the foot of a lady who was being prayed over. I don't know why God drops feathers in church services, but I think it represents what we see in Psalm 91[21], "He will cover you with his feathers, and under his wings you will find refuge." Another time, I was catching a flight from

Atlanta to Washington D.C., and when I got to my seat there was a feather sitting on it. I wouldn't have thought twice about this if I had never seen a supernatural feather before, and I would have just pushed it onto the floor before I sat down; this time I was able to pick it up. I examined it for a few minutes, and then placed it on my leg after I settled in for the flight. I stared at it for a little while, and wondered what it could mean, or if it was even from heaven. It could have just been a feather from one of the airline pillows, but I didn't want to miss an opportunity if God was up to something. I was working on this book at that time, and I heard God say to me that I needed to include some feather stories, so that's where this section of the book, originated. Did God create a feather, and drop it on my seat, or did he just cause a feather to fall from a pillow? I really don't know the answer to that, but he did get my attention, and deliver a message to me; as I write this I am actually sitting on that flight, and I can still see the feather on my leg out of my peripheral vision. I mentioned earlier that I keep a small wooden box on my desk for ministry mementos, and I decided I would take the feather home, and add it to that collection. It might not even be supernatural, but it sure means a lot to me now.

Not long after my first few encounters with the angelic I asked God to make our home a place where angels travelled through on their way to, and from assignments. I wanted our house to be a place angels could hang out in as they waited for their next set of, orders because I was sure it would be a blessing to have a bunch of supernatural beings carry God's presence through the house on a regular basis. Since praying that prayer up until today I can tell you that there has been an increased amount of supernatural activity in our home. We often feel angels moving about, and the measure of God's presence has increased exponentially. It's rare for me to feel God's presence anywhere else as strong as I do in my living room, and there are even times when I can feel his presence pouring out of the house as I get close to the front door. We have even heard testimonies of people who were supernaturally healed a few seconds after walking into our house without anyone praying for them.

I have a theory I want to share with you about how the angelic operate within the spirit realm. I haven't directly observed this for myself, but I think we can infer from a few different scriptures how things play out. Isaiah 55[22] describes the powerfulness of God's word, "so is my word that goes out from my mouth: It will not return to me empty, but will accomplish what I desire, and achieve the purpose for which I sent it." And later it says in Psalm 103[23] that angels "perform his word." I think this literally means that they carry it to completion. Now we already know, and discussed that God can do anything, but since he created the angels to carry out his word, I think that they have a very active role in most of what God does, if not everything. So my theory is that when God speaks, the angelic take hold of his word, and carry it to the one who it was intended. For example, if my theory is correct, if God points down from his throne at a person with cancer, and says "cancer be gone" an angel rushes down to that person's side, and literally removes the cancer. And I think we can even take this a step further, and include the role of the believer in this process as well. When we partner with God by speaking healing into someone's body, I think the angels recognize that partnership, and respond accordingly. We speak on his behalf, we represent Jesus, and just as an ambassador has the authority to speak for the one who sent him, we also have that authority. I haven't yet decided what I believe in regards to followers of Jesus having the ability, or authority to command angels to take actions, but if we speak on God's behalf, then this may actually be even bigger than I realize, especially in the context of the power of words.[24]

I already mentioned that Hebrews 1[25] says that all angels are ministering spirits sent to help those who will inherit salvation. Some people believe that they have the authority to direct angels whenever they are in the course of their ministry. I'm sure they don't think that they can tell an angel to go make them a peanut butter sandwich, but in regards to the work of God, they feel that it is within the authority they have been given by God to use the angels. I haven't ever tried to give any, orders to the angelic, that I know of, but I do think there is some intertwined responsibility. If you are praying for someone who needs a new lung, and you could get an angel to deliver, and make the installation that would be pretty powerful. I have asked God to send angels with new body parts before, but I have never directed an angel to do it myself. I don't think it offends God when we operate out of faith, even if we don't always understand what we are doing, or how we do it. If someone is giving direction to the angels without having the needed authority, the angels probably just ignore them. I don't think it angers God if we make mistakes while trying to work on his behalf; he knows that risk taking involves the possibility of failure, and while he never fails, we often mess up our task along the way. I'm still not entirely sure how to partner with these supernatural beings as I partner with God, but I don't want to criticize others for their theories either. So I'll leave this one up to you to think, and pray about. I'm seeking some revelation in this area myself.

Writing about supernatural beings, and supernatural events is fun, and interesting at the same time. I like to think about all that God has created, and how each piece of that creation plays a role in his master plan. If something as small as the dung beetle has an incredibly important purpose in keeping the earth clean, I think it is fair to say that the angelic host certainly has a much larger role to play. All the encounters people have had with angels in the Bible, some good encounters, and some really bad ones, show us that God has been using them to accomplish a part of his plan since the very beginning. There is really no good reason to think that he isn't still using them today, and that we can't ask him to send the angels down to help us out as we represent him on the earth. Every time I go out to minister somewhere, whether it is in a church, or on the streets, I have made it a routine to ask God for angels to join me on the task. I figure a few thousand angels will always be useful in healing, deliverance, or any other ministry opportunities that pop up. The angelic are powerful beings that carry more of God's presence than our human bodies can endure, so it is likely that their assistance to us helps bring about the miracles we declare when we minister to others. Can God do it all by himself? Of course he can, but he enjoys watching all of us, including the angels, participate in making the world a better place by bringing his kingdom to earth. And honestly I think the angels are probably as interested in us as we are in them. Luke 15[26] tells us that angels rejoice over every sinner who repents, so it stands to reason that they are constantly watching to see how our lives unfold. I wonder if they ask God for permission to interact with humans. It's kind of a funny thing to think about because they have a much better vantage point of the universe than we do, but I think we see a veiled reference to curiosity in Luke 15 as well as 1 Corinthians 4[27]. One thing is for sure; angels will definitely be a topic of discussion when Jesus shows up to have coffee with me.

Endnotes
1. Genesis 3:24
2. Genesis 18:2
3. Exodus 33:2
4. Matthew 4:11
5. Luke 22:43
6. Hebrew 1:14
7. 2 Kings 6:17 (NASB)
8. Revelation 22:8-9
9. Acts 12:7
10. Throughout the book of Revelation.
11. Luke 1:26-31
12. Revelation 10:9
13. Throughout the book of Daniel.
14. Genesis 28:12
15. John 1:51
16. Mark 1:10
17. John 14:12

18. Psalm 104:4, and Hebrews 1:7 (NASB)
19. Acts 2:2-3
20. Luke 3:16
21. Psalm 91:4
22. Isaiah 55:11
23. Psalm 103:20 (NASB)
24. Proverbs 18:21
25. Hebrews 1:14
26. Luke 15:10
27. Luke 15:10, and 1 Corinthians 4:9

Going Deeper

1. Have you ever seen, or interacted with an angel? If so, what was the experience like? If not, how do you think you would react?

---

2. Does the idea of supernatural events happening around you cause any specific feelings, such as fear, or excitement?

---

3. Are you open to God doing anything in your life, even if it is supernatural and unexplainable?

---

4. What is one specific thing you would like God to reveal to you about angelic activity?

Deeper Prayer

Most people don't put much thought into the idea of angels. I tend to think that is a little silly since there is plenty of angelic activity mentioned in the Bible. Below is the prayer I prayed over our home, and over other people's homes, that brought about an increase in angelic activity, pray it for yourself if you would like God to begin sending angels into your home. He's a good daddy, and he loves to give good gifts to his children. He also loves it when we pursue to know more about him and the way he works.

Father, let this place be a place where angels travel through when they move between heaven and earth, and rest while they wait for their next assignment. Just as Jacob saw the angels ascending and descending from heaven, let a staircase also be here for the angels to travel across while carrying out your word.

CHAPTER ELEVEN

GETTING STARTED

Now that you have an understanding of who you are, and what you are supposed to be doing, the next burning question on your mind is probably "how do I get started?" It's actually quite simple, just get out there, and start going for it! Jesus said that all believers will lay hands on the sick, and see them healed[1], so this should be something everyone pursues. I do believe that some are given a special anointing, and are called to specific ministries, but that shouldn't stop anyone else from praying for the sick. It is the job of every Christian to represent Jesus, and healing is something he did everywhere he went[2]. It is one of the core activities he participated in while walking on the earth. But remember that Jesus died for more than just physical sickness. There are a plethora of people who struggle with emotional problems, mental illnesses, and in some cases those problems are influenced by demonic spirits. Some of them are sitting in your church right now, not being ministered to because no one in your church realizes that they are holding the solution to the problem. That's the point of this whole book. Most Christians are not properly equipped to help even the person sitting next to them in church. You can be that solution, you can be the one God flows his power through to touch the lives of those in need. It doesn't matter what it is, you have the authority to push sickness out of the door. You have the authority to command the demons to leave. You have the authority to declare joy where depression has taken root. You have the authority to release peace into lives destroyed by fear. Everything Jesus paid for is available for you to hand out. You just have to reach out, and take hold of it.

Join the prayer team at your church, and start praying for anyone who responds. There are always people in need, and when you make yourself available to pray, people will start coming to you. You might even be the only person on your prayer team who is now equipped to see the sick healed, so pray for everything. And always pray the same way regardless of the problem. Don't think that cancer is harder for God to heal than a broken fingernail. And don't think that when you pray for someone with a terminal disease that you have to pray longer, and harder. You don't. God can heal a headache just as easily as he can make a leg grow out from a stump. Just start going for it, and God will show up, and do his part. When miracles start to happen, they will create an atmosphere of faith and expectation that will eventually spread to others in the congregation. If you don't see a lot of people healed inside the church, than go look for them somewhere else. They are everywhere! Most people won't refuse prayer if you offer it, so when you see someone walking along the street with a cane, go offer to pray. It's a little crazy, and a little bold, but you'll be surprised how often they will stop what they are doing to receive prayer.

God sees who we are now, and also who we can become

Ask God to send people to you who you are equipped to help. Watch out! This one can be interesting because people will start coming to you. I get emails all the time from people who want prayer, and I love it because there is already a sense of expectation for a miracle. And I don't have to go convince a complete stranger to let me pray for them. One of the hardest parts about getting started in this type of ministry is learning to overcome the awkwardness of asking people if they need a miracle. Everyone tends to respond differently, so when someone comes to you looking for a miracle it makes the encounter so much easier. Sometimes our passions make it easier to step out because you can specifically look for people you are passionate about helping. If you have a passion to help people struggling with depression, you should start praying for anyone you know who is depressed. Ask the Holy Spirit to show you the root cause of their depression, and how to pray to get it reversed. It's amazing what God will teach you when you start taking steps of faith to act on his behalf. Tell God you want to see people through his eyes. God sees people differently than we do. He sees who they are now, but he also sees who they can become. He sees the sickness, but he also sees the healed state. I once heard someone say that when you pray for someone don't see the missing arm, see the arm that is missing. Don't see the person as someone who is crippled, you should instead see them as already healed. This isn't some kind of positive thinking routine; it's seeing what God wants for the person, and then getting it for them. God has what we all need, so partner with him, and enjoy the opportunity to deliver his gift to others.

Something else I love to do is to ask God to highlight people to me that he wants to touch, or speak to. People won't always come to the altar for prayer for a variety of different reasons, but if you approach them they will almost always accept prayer, this is especially true when inside a church. I was at a seminar several years ago, and during one of the sessions I noticed someone in the room that looked incredibly familiar to me. I kept thinking that I had met him somewhere before, but I couldn't figure out when, or where. I talked to him at the end of the session, and began to grill him with a ton of questions trying to figure out why he looked so familiar. We concluded that we had never met before, but I was still certain he looked familiar. That evening I spoke to my wife about the experience, and she told me that God was probably highlighting him to me. That was interesting since we already concluded we had never met, and yet I still couldn't get his face out of my head. And what I have learned since then is that anytime I see someone that I have never met who looks familiar to me it is usually God's way of pointing them out. This is a great thing to practice in church because it's easy to scan the crowd for someone that God is highlighting. I will usually look across the church just as the service is starting, and a few more times during the service while I am teaching to see if anyone stands out. God almost always points someone out to me, and then I deliver the message he has for them. Sometimes they have a need, and other times they don't want to talk about it, but in either case I share what I feel like God is saying, offer to pray, and release God's love. What a crazy concept; praying for people at church.

Compassion is not a substitution for expectation

There was another time when I was getting ready to pray for someone, and I was trying to be compassionate as he described to me the pain that he was enduring, and the difficulty of having that particular injury. I heard myself saying things like "wow" and "that's tough," and within that moment I didn't realize that those simple words were actually destroying my faith. Later that evening the Lord told me to never respond to sickness with concern. We empower what we agree with, and what I realized was that my words that night were in some way agreeing with his sickness. Concern is nothing more than worry. No sickness is more powerful than God. No disease can challenge the work that was done on the cross. Every disease must bow at the feet of Jesus. That's the attitude we need to have when praying for the sick. This guy didn't get healed that night, and he left in the same state of pain as he arrived. It's good to have compassion; Jesus was moved with compassion lots of times, so don't think it's bad for your heart to break when you see someone in need. But compassion is more than just feeling sorry for a person's condition. Having a desire to alleviate the person's suffering is also part of being compassionate. But compassion is also not a substitution for expectation. Compassion should move you to pray, and then expectation should take over. It's not good enough to feel sorry for someone, and then pray from a perspective of sorrow; praying from a perspective of authority is always more powerful. Remember your identity when you pray. Remember that you are the light of the world, the salt of the earth, and that you are seated in heavenly places with Christ. You have authority over sickness, disease, and demons, so don't pray from any other perspective.

One thing everyone who prays for the sick needs to learn right away is the importance of understanding that it is always God's will to heal. But for some reason, a reason we really don't know the answer to, sometimes people are not healed. It can be tough when you first start out in this type of ministry because you may go a long time before you see anyone healed. I spent seven months in tenacious pursuit of a healing before the first one happened. Others have prayed for hundreds, or thousands of people before anyone got better. It's easy to start looking for excuses when people are not healed. Let me give you some advice right now; don't do that. Don't look for excuses, or reasons. Your goal should be to see 100% of everyone you pray for get better, but when it doesn't happen you can't blame yourself, and you certainly shouldn't blame the one who is sick. I think this is one of the biggest reasons why churches don't pursue a healing ministry. They don't know how to respond when someone comes up for prayer, and nothing happens. They don't even want to ask the person if they feel better because they already know nothing happened. It can be a little embarrassing if you keep praying, and nothing ever happens. It's easier to just avoid the whole process, so that no one's pride, or self-confidence is negatively affected. There are reasons why people don't get healed. There has to be a reason because if it is God's will, and it doesn't happen, something must be blocking it. Sometimes it's unforgiveness, or some type of sin in the person's life, or just a lack of faith. But for every reason I can think of why someone wouldn't get healed, I can also provide a testimony of someone else in that same situation that did get healed. So I don't put any thought into it when someone I encounter is not made better. I encourage them that it is God's will to heal, and they should keep praying, and believing; then I bless them, and move onto the next person. Another important note on this topic is that you can't carry the burden of someone who isn't healed either. It is really easy to become burdened with someone else's pain, but you can't carry the weight of everyone's sickness. That job belongs to Jesus, and he is really good at it. He alone has the strength to carry the burdens of the world. There's an easy way to remember this; Jesus gets the glory when someone is healed, and Jesus carries the burden when they are not healed. It's not your glory, and it's not your burden, so don't try to carry either.

If you are a pastor you need know that you set the ceiling for what God does in your church. You have been placed in charge of a ministry by God, and he allows you to manage it in your own style, but he will often only move as far as you will allow him. I'm sure you have heard some people say that the Holy Spirit is a gentlemen, and I think that is true most of the time. God rarely forces his will on us, and within the walls of a church he typically leaves the responsibility of stewardship up to the ones he has placed in charge. It can be tough as a pastor to push into new ministry territory when you don't have any past experience in that arena. I suppose it isn't much different from changing careers without all the necessary education. You can easily feel like you're in over your head, and that is all it takes to keep anyone from pursuing the more that God promises. Standing in front of the congregation, and telling them that God wants to heal, and then not seeing anything happen can be demoralizing. The truth is that some pastors have lost their churches over smaller issues, so I understand when there is some apprehension to expand the focus of a ministry into an area that can easily have the appearance of getting out of control. Jesus never promised that ministry would be a clean business. He actually promised the opposite. I grew up seeing miracles, and I still didn't pursue it until much later in my life. I knew what was possible, and I saw with my own eyes what God could do, and yet I waited a long time to take the first step. I wonder sometimes how many lives would have been different if I wouldn't have waited so long. I've read the stories of pastors who have been fired from their denomination because they refused to stop teaching about supernatural healing. I know at least one of those pastors who has a thriving healing ministry today all because he refused to worry about what everyone else thought, and decided instead to believe God's word. It's easy for me to tell you to just take God at his word. But this is something you can't take my word for; you have to step out in faith, and watch God work.

I pray for people everywhere I go. I try to keep an eye out for canes, wheelchairs, braces, or any other visual clue that someone needs a miracle. It's a little awkward approaching a complete stranger in an airport lounge, and asking them if they want prayer. People tend to be automatically hesitant when anyone offers something to them; I think that's a result of the telemarketing world we live in, but it's not going to keep me from getting them what they need. I saw a guy in the airport with a brace on his wrist. His hand was badly swollen, and it looked like it was a fairly recent injury. He had a drink in his other hand, and was placing the cold glass on his injured hand, probably to reduce the swelling, and numb the pain. It was a perfect opportunity because he was obviously in pain, so I walked over to talk to him. I think he was a little surprised that I just sat down next to him, and started a conversation. I suppose I would be surprised if someone did the same thing to me. He told me how he injured his hand, and I shared with him that I see miracles every week, and I could get him a miracle if he wanted one. Sadly, he didn't want me to pray. So I told him to have a nice day, and went back to my own business. I don't let those situations discourage me because I know that Jesus was turned away from entire regions. In Mark 5[3], just after he freed a demon possessed man "the people began to plead with Jesus to leave their region." I don't know why anyone would ask you to leave after seeing a miracle, especially one that involved a man who had been tormented for a long time. But it happens all the time. So I try to keep going for it wherever I'm at, and I don't get upset when people refuse prayer. If anything, I feel a little sorry for them because they just missed an opportunity to have an encounter with Jesus. I don't always stop for everyone I see in need. Sometimes I'm focused on other tasks and I don't make the time. Sometimes I'm just tired. There's no good excuse for it, but it happens, and one of my goals is to never walk past anyone in need without stopping to give them what I have. I'll get there eventually.

I'm telling you that you need to get out there, and start going for it, so I want to make sure you are properly equipped; I'm going to show you a simple way to pray for people. There are lots of ways to pray, and this is just an example that you can use to get started, but there are a couple of variables you should be aware of. First, you don't have to ask God to heal anyone. Ok, that sounds a little strange, so I'll expound on it. Jesus already gave you the authority to represent him on the earth. When we look at the scriptures there is never an example of Jesus asking the father to come heal someone, or to get rid of a demon. He simply declares, or commands, and the problem goes away. In one case he didn't say anything at all, and a woman was healed of a long time disease[4]. A good analogy I heard somewhere went something like this: imagine for a minute that you were standing in front of God, and he said "I want to give you one hundred dollars." And then you responded by saying "God can I have one hundred dollars?" That would be a silly response, and I think God would probably have a strange expression on his face. It doesn't make sense to ask for something someone already gave you. We have already been given authority, so when we pray we don't have to say things like "please God, heal this person of asthma." Instead, we can simply say "asthma get out," or "leg grow in the name of Jesus," or "tumor shrivel up, and die right now in Jesus name." Do you see the difference? One is a petitionary prayer asking God to give something he has already placed in our toolbox. The other is an authoritative command to the body, or sickness, ordering the situation to be changed; we don't command God, we command the body. And it's no different if you come across someone possessed with an evil spirit. You don't have to ask God to make the demon leave, you can command it to leave on your own because of the authority you have been given. There are times for petitionary prayers, but when it comes to healing I almost always use command prayers to get the job done.

The model is fairly simple. Start out by finding out what's wrong, then start praying. Your prayers don't need to be long, or include big words that make you sound holy. Just use a short, simple, childlike prayer. Remember, kids believe what their father tells them. The healing doesn't depend on you, it depends on God; there is no reason for you to spend 30 minutes contending for a healing. Spend about 15, or 20 seconds commanding healing into the body, and then have the person check themselves out to see if anything has changed. It's good to ask questions about the pain level, or mobility to get a sense for what God is doing. If they had trouble walking have them walk around for a few minutes to see if it's better. The key here is to have them try to do something they couldn't do before. I was praying for a guy with a broken wrist, and once I saw that some of the mobility had returned I had him remove the brace, so he could test out the strength of the wrist to see how much pressure it could endure. First he rotated it around a few times, and then he started squeezing his arm to see if there was any more pain. These are exciting moments for the one praying, and the one receiving prayer. It's a boost to everyone's faith, and it makes you want to immediately go find someone else to pray over. Sometime they are healed after that first prayer, but if they are not healed, go for it again. Hit it with another 15 seconds of prayer, and repeat the process. It's also important to listen to the Holy Spirit while you are praying.

The Holy Spirit will often give you words to pray, or reveal what the root cause of the sickness is, so you can pray more effectively. I will generally pray for anything that randomly pops into my head especially if it's really odd because I'm not trying to figure out what is wrong in that moment. I'm not concerned about how things are connected, I'm just going for healing, and if the Holy Spirit drops something on me, I put it out there. Jesus did what the Father did[5], and the Holy Spirit reveals to us what the Father is up to[6]; listening is part of the partnership. I usually pray two, or three times like this before I stop. If there is any improvement at all I keep going for it, but if nothing has changed I give them some quick advice. Unfortunately some people don't get healed. We talked about that a little already, but let me share with you a great way how to handle the situation when nothing happens. The best thing you can do is encourage the person that God wants to heal them, and even though it didn't happen right now it doesn't mean God is not going to take care of it. Never tell them that they don't have enough faith, and don't think that about yourself either. Bless them, and then move onto the next person who is waiting. Most people don't actually expect anything to happen when you pray anyways, so if they aren't healed it's not a major devastating blow. But it can be difficult because part of you wants to keep praying until they are healed. The practical reality is that if there are 100 people waiting to be prayed for you can't spend 30 minutes with each one. Of course every situation is different, and you need to follow God's direction, but this basic model will give you a place to start. And sometimes the Holy Spirit will even share supernatural information with you before you pray.

1 Corinthians 12[7] gives us a list of some of the spiritual gifts available to all believers for use in expanding the kingdom of heaven. I say some because I don't think these verses were meant to be an all-inclusive, or an exhaustive list of everything God can, and will do through his partners. Of the listed gifts there are a few that work very well in tandem with healing. One of those is words of knowledge[8]. If you have never seen someone operate in the gifts of the Holy Spirit before, it could be a little shocking if a minister gets on the stage, and

starts declaring the sicknesses that people in the room are affected by. You might hear something like "someone here has cancer in the left lung," or "there is a woman who is blind in the left eye." Receiving words of knowledge is one of the ways we can hear what the Father is speaking. God likes to reveal to us what he is doing, so we can partner with him. A word of knowledge is when the Holy Spirit supernaturally tells you something that you couldn't otherwise know if he hadn't shared it with you. This could apply to anything; an event in someone's life, a problem someone is struggling with, or a sickness someone is enduring are just a few examples. The key here is that it has to be something you didn't already know, or can't perceive using your regular senses. If you see someone with a neck brace on, you can't walk up, and say "God just told me you had a neck injury." That's silly. But often times, during services where healing is expected, or anticipated, the Holy Spirit will begin to reveal injuries that the father wants to heal. God doesn't reveal these injuries to us just for fun, or just to share information. He gives us the information, so that we can release the word for someone's healing. We even see people healed sometimes immediately after the word is given without anyone praying for them.

You can receive these words in a variety of ways, there is no limit to how the Holy Spirit can, and will speak to you when you are willing to be used. The primary way that I receive words of knowledge is by feeling something in my body that is not normal. What I mean by that is the Holy Spirit will cause me to feel a pain, or a sensation in an area of the body that someone has an injury. I'm in pretty good health, so I don't have to worry about if what I am feeling is my pain, or someone else's, but if you are someone who has physical injuries you'll need to keep track of what your own pain is, so you don't get anything mixed up. Another common way to receive a word is by thinking it. This is also sometimes referred to as a mental impression, or a random thought. If the word pancreas randomly pops into your head, and it's not something you were already thinking about, than it is probably a word of knowledge for someone who needs a healing in their pancreas.

The way I gauge this is, if it is something I don't know anything about, or something I don't usually think about, then I make a note of it. Some people can actually see words appear like a teleprompter superimposed over someone, or over another object like a wall, or floor. A word like suicide could appear over someone's forehead; faith for sharing these ones is pretty easy because seeing a word floating in the air is not normal. One more way I want to describe is that people will sometimes see an image in their mind, or just floating in the air like a TV screen that visually shows the problem, or situation. This could be an image of a broken toe, or maybe even a car wreck for example. There are other ways to receive words, and regardless of how the Holy Spirit speaks to you, just remember that he is sharing with you, so that someone can be healed. One side note, if the Holy Spirit reveals something to you that could be embarrassing, or humiliating to the person it is for, don't get on the stage, and scream it out. Go find that person, and minister to them privately. We don't use the gifts to beat people down; we build them up by delivering God's healing through an attitude of love.

These words don't just come during a church service, you can get them anytime. I keep notes on my phone, and jot down anything I receive during the day, and then I release it whenever I have the opportunity. Sometimes the words are for the person sitting next to us on a train, or walking past us in a grocery store aisle. Paying attention to what Holy Spirit is speaking throughout our day can give us the opportunity to change lives everywhere we go. Sharing a word of knowledge is one of the ultimate risk taking adventures. Standing in front of a group of people, large, or small, to share what God is saying can be nerve racking; especially the first time. Sometimes we miss it, and sometimes people don't respond, but we do it anyways because it is an act of obedience, and the more we step out in faith, the more God will use us in that way. When you have the opportunity to share, simply describe what you are feeling, sensing, seeing, etc., but don't expound on what you receive, just release it, and see if it makes sense to anyone. I once had a word where I felt a pain in my right forearm from the wrist all the way to the elbow. I knew it was a word for healing when I received it, but I started to think about what it could be. I was thinking maybe it is carpel tunnel, or it could be a knife wound;, but the Holy Spirit told me to just say what I felt, and not try to interpret it. When I shared it a little later someone immediately responded, and was healed a few minutes afterwards. Just put it out there, and pray for the ones that respond.

I love to pray for people, but it wasn't always that way. I used to be afraid to pray in public because I was worried about sounding funny, or not praying long enough, or not using the right words. I was concerned about what other people thought to the point that I let it keep me from being myself. But now I'll pray for anyone, anywhere, at any time. I don't care who is watching, or what they think. If anything, I think God gets more glory when someone is healed in a public place than when it happens at a church altar. There's something about watching someone celebrate on a sidewalk that gets everyone's attention. So now I love to pray. I love to see miracles, it's the greatest thing I have ever been involved in, and it never gets boring. I get excited every time another person gets healed. Not because I'm surprised that it happened, but because I'm happy God showed up. When you first start seeing miracles, it will surprise you. You'll be shocked when the first one happens. And then it will start happening often enough that it will become a normal part of your life. A friend told me once that you shouldn't be surprised when you see a miracle. You should be surprised when you don't see it happen. You should have so much expectation that you are shocked when a healing doesn't occur. That's the perspective you should minister from. Getting started is really easy; you just have to start praying for people. The more people you pray for, the more will get healed. If you don't pray for anyone it will never happen. The worst that could happen is that someone walks away in the same condition that they came; but even in that situation they still receive something because they'll know that they are loved.

God loves risk takers, so just get out there, and start doing it.

Endnotes
1. Mark 16:18
2. Luke 6:19
3. Mark 5:17
4. Luke 8:43-44
5. John 5:19
6. John 16:15
7. 1 Corinthians 12:4-11
8. 1 Corinthians 12:8

Going Deeper

1. Is there anything keeping you from pursuing a life of miracles right now?

2. Does the idea of representing Jesus everywhere you go scare or excite you?

3. Where is the first place you want to try representing the supernatural love of Jesus? A restaurant, movie theater, somewhere else?

4. What is the most burning question you have right now?

Deeper Prayer

The most common question we ever receive after teaching a room full of people about how to minister supernaturally is, "now what?" There is often a desire to do something with what they have just learned, mixed with a trepidation about actually doing it. Our answer is always the same, "go do it!" Step out in faith, use the tools God has given to you, and go change the world! Holy Spirit will always be there to help you along the way, here's a great prayer to pray for his help:

Holy Spirit, I want to be used more by you to change the world around me, and to share your love with others. Please give me the boldness to minister to those in need, the discernment to know how to minister effectively, and the same compassion Jesus has for every person I meet. I don't really know what I am doing. I am willing to step out, but I need your help.

CHAPTER TWELVE

TESTIMONIES

Being a missionary to the nation's capital is incredible. Our absolute favorite place to minister is in the laundromat parking lot in Southeast Washington D.C. that I mentioned earlier. I love going to this location, and loving on the people we see because it is an opportunity to reach the members of society that many others have forgotten about, or ignored. Jesus loves outcasts, and so do I. Our model is simple. We setup a table on one end of this parking lot, and offer granola bars, water, and lemonade (or something warm during the winter months) to anyone who wants it. This is a simple offering that has two purposes. Many of the people we encounter on these days need some hydration because of all the alcohol in their systems, and the granola bars provide a little nutrition for their bodies. But our primary goal is to use this offering as a connection point. People will come to us to looking for a snack, and a drink, then we offer to pray for them as well. A few refuse prayer, but most will share about a need, and we are given the opportunity to connect them to their heavenly Father who loves them so much. So we take time every week, unless we are out of town, to spend a few hours in a parking lot with addicts, dealers, prostitutes, and anyone else who happens through the area. What's so amazing is that God shows up with us every week, and touches the lives of the people we encounter. Miracles have become a normal part of the weekly activities in the parking lot, so much so that some of the people who are regularly there talk about what is happening. After praying for a handful of people one morning, Lauren took some granola bars into the laundromat to hand them out. On her way, she overheard a group of guys, who were actively smoking marijuana, having a theological discussion about what we were doing. It's exciting to know that we are having direct, and indirect impacts in a community that has been largely forgotten for many years.

On one particular morning, we met a man named Garland, who would sweep up the parking lot, and keep it clean to earn some extra money. We were watching him for a few minutes, and noticed he was limping as he moved, and he wasn't moving very fast. As he came to our table for some water, I asked him what was wrong with his leg, and he began to tell us about how he had injured his knee, and that it was always in pain as a result. I told him that we could take care of it for him, then I placed my hand on his knee, said a quick prayer, and asked him to test it out. I wish you could have seen the expression on his face. Many times, we can tell that God is healing someone simply by the look on their face. The normal expression that was on their face before the prayer suddenly turns into one of shock as they feel the power of God go through them, or feel something change in their body. The expression on Garland's face gave it all away. But his statement was even better. He moved his leg around for a few seconds then shouted out, "what the f*** is going on around here?" That's a real, raw, response. It's a phrase that would offend most Christians, but it didn't faze us one bit. We told him that Jesus had touched his leg, and he responded, "that's some spooky sh**!" The other thing about this man is that he was drunk, or high, when he first came over to us, but became completely sober at the same time he was healed. We have seen this sobering up effect occur on many occasions as the presence of God saturated the person standing in front of us. It's incredible how God will, not only heal the physical injury, but also clear the mind, so they know what is happening. We chatted with Garland for a few more minutes, then he went back to sweeping the parking lot. But now, he was moving twice as fast, and without a limp!

One of our favorite parking lot stories started about 20 feet away from our table, as a man wearing a dark overcoat cautiously approached us to see what we were doing. We noticed that he was watching from a distance, and that he wasn't planning on coming any closer. I grabbed a few granola bars, walked out to meet him, and introduced myself. Do you remember the story in the book of Mark[1] when Jesus asked the demon possessed man for his name? When he replied, it wasn't the man speaking, it was one of the demons inside of him that answered Jesus. Well, after introducing myself to this man in the parking lot, the demon inside of him also replied. But his name wasn't legion, it was undertaker. He stood there looking at me with a blank stare. His hands and feet were badly swollen from, what I later found out, was Gout. He wouldn't let me pray for him, so I blessed him, and he went on his way. He came to us again a few weeks later, but this time he came all the way to the table. He repeated the same introduction as before, as the demon inside of him wanted to make sure we knew who was in control of his life. But that was all about to change because on this day, he let us pray for him. We commanded the demon to leave him, and prayed for complete healing over his body. He left, and we didn't see him again for over a year. Then, one day, a man walks up in brightly colored clothes and starts chatting with some other people in the parking lot. He had a big smile on his face, and the others in the parking lot greeted him by his name, T.J. There was something familiar about him, but I couldn't quite figure out what it was. Then I shook his hand, and in that instant I knew this was the man who used to introduce himself as the undertaker. He wasn't the undertaker anymore. That demon was gone. And the swollen hands and feet were gone as well. I don't know why we hadn't seen him for so long, but I am happy that he was set free from the spirit that had control over his life. We see him on a regular basis now, and continue to pray for him to have employment, his own home, and full restoration of everything the enemy has stolen from him.

Testimonies get me fired up. I love to hear about what God is doing all over the world because it shows how much he loves to encounter his creation. There really is nothing like a supernatural encounter with God that can shift a person's perspective into seeing a new reality. It doesn't matter if it is a physical healing, salvation, deliverance, or any other supernatural encounter with God; every single encounter is powerful, and worth sharing about because it gives us a glimpse of the Father's heart.

I was speaking at a church in Southern California, and after teaching the congregation about healing, I invited those who needed healing to come forward for prayer. Richard had been standing in the back of the room listening to my teaching, and he was the first one to come to the front for prayer. I had never met him before, but his story was similar to what we often hear. He told me that he was recently diagnosed with cancer, and that he had three small tumors in his lower abdomen. He also told me that his life wasn't right with God, and that he needed to get that taken care of as well. I suspect he was concerned that the cancer would get the best of him, so getting his salvation squared away was an important step for him to take. There was also a sincerity in his voice that told me he really wanted to make a change in his life. We took a few moments for him to surrender his life to God, which is always the greater miracle, and then I commanded the tumors to disappear. At this point, I had never seen cancer healed in someone I prayed for, I had heard a lot of testimonies, but never saw it with my own eyes. I wasn't sure what was going to happen. I wasn't sure if there would be any change. There was a man standing in front of me, who was in need of a miracle, and in that moment, he needed Jesus to touch his life. And that is exactly what Jesus did.

I asked him to feel the area where the tumors were, so we would know if anything had changed. He took a few seconds, moved his hand around in a few different areas, and declared that he couldn't find the tumors! They were gone! The lumps that were present just a few seconds earlier had completely disappeared! I later learned that Richard continued to attend, and serve in, this church on a weekly basis. God performed two miracles that day. First, Richard's soul was saved, he became a new creation, and the trajectory of his life was changed. Second, a horrible disease was removed from his body, along with the fear of what it could have led to. I'm just glad I was there to witness what God wanted to do.

Ministering in the supernatural brings new discoveries about the goodness of God on an almost daily basis. One of the things I think we all tend to learn as we go down this road is that God is not limited to what we think he can do; he can do so much more! We get so excited about physical healing that it's easy to forget about the other needs God wants to meet. We were at a meeting a few years ago, chatting with some people after the service was over, and a lady approached me to share a testimony of something incredible God had done for her. She started by sharing that I probably didn't remember her, which I didn't, and then she began to recount a story about how I prayed a financial blessing over her a year earlier, and since that time, she had been living in Hawaii for free, paid off all her debts, and was in the process of buying a second home! Seriously?! That's incredible! I immediately asked her to pray for me because, who wouldn't want to live in Hawaii at no cost for a full year?

We have also had several people approach us in the parking lot to receive prayer for a place to live. We often encounter people experiencing homelessness, or those who are currently living in a shelter, who need a permanent place to live; a place to call their own. It's a tough situation to be in, but we know that God's goodness is not determined by the difficulty level of our situation. If he will give one person a rent free place to live in Hawaii for a year, he will certainly provide a home for someone dealing with homelessness. In one instance, a lady reported to us that she received a call from her case worker on the same day that we prayed for her, and the case worker told her that a house was available. She picked up the keys to her new home just a few hours after our prayer. Then, the following week, her case worker drove her to the parking lot, so she could inform us of what had happened. This same testimony has been repeated multiple times as people who have had no permanent place to live were able to transition into a home of their own after God intervened. And we have also received reports of people getting new jobs after being healed from injuries that kept them from being able to work.

One of the first physical miracles that occurred in the parking lot was the healing of a man's back that had been in pain for many years. Del used to be a driver for a delivery service, but was unable to work because his back problems prevented him from sitting in the vehicle or carrying heavy objects. We didn't know he was a driver at first, we only knew he had back pain. So we prayed, and God healed him. Then we prophesied that he would have a job as a driver. Del returned the following week to tell us that his back was still healed, and that he was hired to drive a truck again! Del experienced two miracles in less than a week, and if that is where the story ended, it would be more than worthy of sharing. But there is more. More than a year later, Del came walking back into the parking lot, and took a few minutes to update us on his life. He had continued to work as a driver, and even received a promotion to a better position with that company, but he then received an opportunity to work in the engineering department of Howard University!

Del went from being unemployed with an injury, to being employed and promoted in one job, to being offered an even better job at a local university. He told us that he used to work as an engineer in this same university but was laid off in the late 1990's. And now, he had his old job back. You may remember the story I told in chapter three about a young man's legs being healed. His story was similar to Del's in that he could not work because of his injury. He returned a few weeks after his miraculous healing to tell us that, since he was able to stand on his feet all day, he was working again. We still see him about once a month, and I'm always quick to ask about his legs, to which he always replies by dancing, jumping, or running around to show off what God did in his life.

And you know what? These types of miracles can happen anywhere. They can happen in the aisle of the local grocery store, they can happen in a school hallway, they can happen in a hospital room, and they can even happen inside of a church. God is not limited to when and where he will show up because he is inside of every believer. If you are there, a miracle can happen. We like to experiment with blending this miraculous lifestyle into events that would not normally have a spiritual component. My status as a veteran has opened up a few doors in the veteran sphere that has allowed us to be part of medical and job fairs that are focused on serving the veteran population. Supernatural ministry is not a common element within military ranks, or at military focused events, but that's exactly why we like being a part these events. It makes us stand out in a unique way, and adds a greater degree of excitement as people with no expectation for a miracle experience something miraculous. We were at one of these veteran job fairs, not to hire anyone, but to provide a support service for those looking for jobs. Our goal was to prophetically speak into the lives of the veterans, and pray for healing for anyone with injuries. The response from one man, when we asked him if he had any pain in his body, was a poignant reminder of our audience that day; he said, "I was in the army for 20 years, of course I have pain in my body." A few of his friends were with him, and they watched as God healed his back and took away the pain. This man came looking for a job, and received a miracle!

I love sharing testimonies because I find that the stories about what Jesus has already done in someone else's life builds faith for others to believe for miracles in their own lives. What God has done for one person, he will certainly do for another. I mentioned in an earlier chapter that Revelation 19:10 describes the testimony of Jesus as the spirit of prophecy. When we tell the stories about what Jesus has done, it can become a prophetic declaration for what he will do again in the future. He wants to heal, he wants to set free, he wants to bring everyone into an amazing relationship with him. He wants to do it again, and again, and again. We have seen people experience supernatural healing after watching a testimony video. We have seen people healed after hearing someone else's miracle story. There is something about testimonies that attracts the presence of God. I once heard someone say that heaven is attracted to itself. It's this idea that heaven takes notice when we talk about what Jesus is doing. The more we talk about it, the more he shows up. God loves performing miracles, and he loves hearing us tell the stories about what he did. Miracles and testimonies have become normal in our lives, and they can become normal in your life as well.

Endnotes
1. Mark 5:9

Going Deeper

1. What is one testimony you could share with others that would inspire them to have greater faith?

----

2. Was there anything in this chapter that caused your own faith to increase?

----

3. Is there anything you want to see God do, that you have never seen before?

Deeper Prayer

Our lives can be a testimony to the goodness of Jesus simply by being his hands and feet everywhere we go. When we have love in our hearts for every person who stands in front of us, or crosses our path, we can release what they need for their lives in that very moment. I find myself constantly praying for more love, and for a greater revelation of his desire to see the kingdom of God fully established on the earth. Pray this prayer with me, and become a living testimony for Jesus:

Holy Spirit, show me what you want me to see. Lead me to the people you want me to minister to. Help me to be more sensitive to your voice, and your direction in my life. I want to be used by you in the fullness of who I was created to be. I want my life to be a living sacrifice to you, and a living testimony of how good you are, so everyone around me will want to know you.

EPILOGUE

I started this book out talking about the identity of every believer on the planet. I believe that once Christians understand who they are they can quickly take on the role that God has given them. A miracle lifestyle is not just for a handful of people, it is for everyone who follows Christ. Powerless Christianity is pointless, and if you're living a Christian lifestyle that is boring, and mundane you are not moving in tandem with God. It's easy to end up on a plateau. It's easy to become comfortable. A lot of pastors, and church elders end up in that position when their churches become large, and stable enough to sustain the ministry. It is easy to think that you have "arrived" at that point, but the reality is that there is always more of God available to the ones who are hungry enough to go after it. Your identity in Christ is a major key in understanding the role you play on the earth. Jesus's sacrifice on the cross fully paid for salvation, physical healing, emotional healing, and deliverance, so that we can partner with him. Your partnership with Christ gives you the authority to represent him, and speak on his behalf as you act like a kid by taking risk to fulfill the mandate he has given to all of us. He will send angels to help you, and as you get a taste of what he has made available to you, you will find yourself addicted to releasing his presence everywhere you go, and then asking for more. It's a constant cycle of releasing, and receiving. We give away what God gives to us, and then we go back to the throne to be replenished, not so that we can keep it for ourselves, but so that we can give it away once again.

If you're not hungry, you need to get hungry real fast. If you are not hungry for more of what God has for you, you will be limited to what you can access. You have access to everything he has, but you have to go, and take it, and it is hunger that drives us to the point of grabbing hold of the resources he has made available to us. Jesus said in that "From the days of John the Baptist until now, the kingdom of heaven has been subjected to violence, and violent people have been raiding it.[1]" I used to be completely confused by this verse. I once thought it meant someone was attacking heaven, but that didn't make any sense because the last crew that tried to take over heaven was kicked out. The amplified Bible expounds on this verse with a note that "a share in the heavenly kingdom is sought with most ardent zeal, and intense exertion." It's not that an enemy of God is violently stealing from heaven, but rather that the tenacious believers in the kingdom are grabbing hold of what is available, and pulling it into the realm of earth. Jesus said ask, seek, and knock[2]; almost as if he was saying that asking wasn't good enough by itself. You have to ask, and then ask some more, then start knocking, and seeking until the answer comes. I think that hunger drives us to be a little more tenacious. There's a rule about grocery shopping that you should never go to the store when you are hungry because you tend to buy a lot more food than you would if you had recently eaten. That hunger drives you to pile more food into the basket because your body is screaming to be fed. If you go to God with no hunger you aren't going to leave with a very full basket. If you are already satisfied with everything you have you won't have the tenacious desire to fill up the basket until it is overflowing. I have often prayed that God would make me hungry, that I would never be satisfied with what he had given me because I want to live a life of continual increase. I like to pray similar prayers over others, and ask God to give them an insatiable hunger for more of him. I have learned that when people are that hungry they won't stop seeking, they won't stop knocking, and they won't stop asking. That's exactly where God wants you.

There is nothing that Jesus didn't pay for. Chris Gore likes to say that we should "go get Jesus everything he paid for." I love that statement because there is so much the Church isn't going after, and I feel like that attitude makes Jesus' sacrifice a little less important. If no pastor ever told anyone about the death of Jesus, salvation would lose some of its meaning. But when we tell the story of what Jesus did, and then invite others to be a part of what he is still doing it brings more glory to the sacrifice. The same is true for healing, or casting out demons, or restoring the outcasts of society, or even raising the dead. Jesus paid for a lot more than we have been willing to pursue, and that needs to end now. He told the disciples "Heal the sick, raise the dead, cleanse those who have leprosy, drive out demons[3]," and that mandate still stands today. But it's not about what you have been mandated, or, ordered to do. It's not about grudgingly complying just because God said to do it. I picture a kid dragging their feet as they inch toward their bed after their dad told them it was time to go to sleep. This is not the image of how we should respond. If anything it should be the exact opposite. We should be excited that we have an opportunity to be a part of what God is doing on the earth today. We have this great opportunity to go out, and grab hold of everything Jesus paid for, and that's amazing! If you can't get excited about miracles than you need to come hang out with me for a few hours; I'll guarantee when we are finished you will be fired up!

Angels can help you, ask God to send them with you, and you'll soon begin to recognize when they are present. I mentioned that I think that some angels don't have assignments because we aren't asking for them. The idea that we have a guardian angel following us around everywhere we go might be true, but somehow I don't think an angel can stay gainfully employed sitting in an office building watching us type all day. It seems to me that they have a lot more they could offer, and I would hate to get to heaven, and find out that I had angelic armies standing by that were never used. So I ask for them, and I have learned how to recognize when they show up, and when they are in the room. But don't just ask God to send the angels, ask him to open up your eyes to see into that realm. I believe that we are more effective when we can see everything going on around us. If you can see what the angels are doing then you know exactly what God is up to because they are carrying out his word. And it doesn't have to be limited to angels. Give all your senses to God for his use. Tell him you want to hear what is happening in heaven. Ask him to let you smell the fragrances from his throne room. God will use anything you give to him, so don't be surprised when you start hearing the footsteps of angels as they come down off the staircase, and walk across your floor. Don't be shocked when your house smells differently during prayer time. It's a little weird at first, but you'll get used to it pretty quick, and once it starts you won't want it to stop.

I've warned you before, and I'll warn you again, this lifestyle is addictive. I see it all the time when I take new people out with me to pray for the sick. All it takes is one miracle, and they are hooked for life. Even people who are skeptical about supernatural healings get fired up when they see God show up, and do something they didn't believe was possible. Actually, people in this group probably get fired up even more than others. There's something about seeing a miracle right in front of your eyes that changes the way you think. I try to imagine how the people in Israel responded when Jesus routinely healed thousands. I wonder if the crowds following close behind were shouting, and clapping as sight was restored, or cripples got up, and walked for the first time in their lives. Watching Jesus move through the crowds must have been amazing. But we don't have to imagine what it looked like, or what people's responses were; we can see it with our own eyes. I love watching the facial expressions that crop up on a face after they realize the problem they used to have doesn't exist anymore. Sometimes it's a look of shock. Other times people burst into tears as they are overwhelmed by the love of God. We've even seen people dance on the side of the street in celebration for receiving a new hip. Watching God work is one of the most amazing things I have ever been a part of, and I wouldn't trade it for anything else. I had a Top Secret clearance for two decades, and was involved in some very cool military operations, but all of that pales in comparison to what I get to do now. I'm addicted for life, and you will be too once you get started.

One of the areas I struggled with when I started pushing into supernatural ministry was that I didn't understand what different manifestations of God's presence meant. I didn't know why my hands would get hot when I prayed, or why I would feel a flame on my head. I couldn't find any books to help me figure any of it out, but I eventually realized that everyone has a different experience with God, and while there are some common elements of heat, and electricity it doesn't always happen the same way. Some people don't feel anything at all, and are still mightily used, so don't put your faith in what you do, or don't feel. The Holy Spirit is the best teacher you can ever have, so if you start to feel, see, or sense something that is not normal for you, ask the Holy Spirit to teach you what it means. God wants us to effectively use the gifts he gives, and will teach us how to use them, and what they mean. I usually learn by asking, and then experimenting with my new knowledge. The Holy Spirit will reveal something to me, and then I will go off, and start putting my new knowledge into practice. I think this is the norm with humans who operate in the supernatural realm. This lifestyle is one big experiment that requires constant risk to push into new areas. I'm used to praying for people, and I'll do it at the drop of a hat, so I don't even see that as risk anymore. But when the Holy Spirit drops a new gift in my lap I go right back to the risk mode of getting the courage to put it to use. I didn't used get a lot of prophetic words for people, so when one came it took a little extra boldness to share it. But just like with healing, every time I step out God brings increase. Ask the Holy Spirit for help, he'll show up, and teach you a few things.

I talked a little bit about feathers randomly appearing, angels showing up to help with your ministry, and other manifestations like heat, and electricity, and now I'd like to end this book with one more story that I think speaks to God's creativity. This one is about supernatural glitter; sometimes called gold dust. This is pretty cool. A few years back my wife went to visit her parents, and while she was gone they attended a church service to hear a guest speaker talk about some of the same stuff you've been reading about in this book. When she came home she told me a story about how glitter appeared on her hands while she was worshipping God during that service. I had never heard of that before. I don't ever remember seeing anything like that in my dad's ministry, and though I wasn't skeptical it honestly didn't interest me. A few days later she showed me her hands at the end of a service in our home church, and I could clearly see a few flakes of glitter not on her hand, but actually under the skin. That was cool, but I still didn't get excited. I'm not really sure why it didn't excite me, but it probably had something to do with my lack of hunger. Truth be told my wife started getting hungry before I did, and it was some of her experiences that I think stirred my spirit up enough to start moving in this direction. This glitter experience continued for a few months, and then one day while I was praying I looked down, and saw a single flake of glitter on my big toe. I asked God if that was him, and then it disappeared. I had thought that maybe there was a piece of glitter already on the floor that had become stuck to my toe, but I realized in that quick second that it was from God.

I felt a little foolish after that, and decided if anything out of the, ordinary ever happened again I would just assume it was God until proven otherwise. That wasn't the end of the glitter experiences. It kept growing, and before I knew it glitter was showing up on my hands too. One night after church we went back to our car, and found glitter sprinkled all over the dashboard. Really? The dashboard? Why would God put glitter in our car while we were in church? This happened on a couple of different occasions, and I have learned to welcome whatever God is doing, especially if it seems a little strange. Other times glitter has appeared all over the stage, speakers, and floor of our church. I remember at the end of a small group session one night my wife mentioned that she had glitter on her hands. A few others came over to see it, and then they started examining their own hands to find they had a little glitter as well. All over the room I kept hearing exciting proclamations of "I have glitter too!" I think glitter is God's way of prettying us up. Women have makeup that includes small specks of glitter to add to their beauty, so maybe God's glitter is designed to make us look a little better, or maybe it's just his way of saying "I love you." I don't really know why God sprinkles glitter all over the floor, or why he creates feathers, and gives them away as gifts. We can come up with a reasonable meaning that makes sense to us, but at the end of the day I think God just loves to create, and enjoys lavishing his love on us, and maybe showing off. It's one of the ways he spends time with us.

It's always fun to spend time with people we enjoy being around. There are some people who light up a room with their personality, their presence in the room can literally change the atmosphere. I recently attended an interview, and book signing event with a famous author, and I was intrigued by the people who were in the room. There were the typical fans of course jockeying to get the best seat, or the best spot in line at the signing table. And then the atmosphere in the room changed when a former Presidential candidate walked in with his wife. There was a visible awe on people's faces as they walked to their seats. The same thing happened when famous news reporters, and foreign ambassadors showed up. None of them had any role to play in the event. They were simply there to attend like everyone else, but their very presence in the room shifted the atmosphere. Something similar happens when God shows up; something better actually. When he walks into a room, when his presence fills the house the change in the atmosphere isn't just perceived, it is tangible. I know comparing a few famous people to God isn't a very good comparison, but there's a point to be made here. Being in the same room with God is the best place you can be. I tried to paint you a picture of what it is like to soak in

God's presence. I think that the more time we spend in his presence, the more of his presence rubs off on us. And if we do it often enough we'll find ourselves carrying that presence everywhere we go. The room won't light up because we are there, it will light up because his presence is on us. What good is it to be someone's partner if you never spend any time with him? We don't know everything he is doing, but simply being in his presence reminds us that he is with us, and that we are not working on our own.

Partnering with God has a lot of those moments where you don't know why he is doing something, but you're just happy to be part of it. I really can't imagine life differently now. I think about where I was a few years ago, and compare that to what I am doing now, and the first word that comes to my mind is wow. I find myself thanking God on a regular basis for giving me such an incredible opportunity. It's a position I could never earn on my own merits. I think that's the best part. God chooses us based on what he sees in us, and not what we see in ourselves. We don't have to have a perfect theology to be used; we just have to be willing. He will smooth out the rough edges along the way. And we don't have to be perfect either. Don't fall into the trap of thinking that you have to attain perfection before you can be used. That's a trick the enemy uses to keep us from reaching our full potential. He used the same trick on Adam, and Eve, and convinced them to think that God was lying[4], or at the very least that God was wrong. And it worked perfectly. They fell for the trap that started us all down this path. Jesus didn't lie when he said the sick would be healed through us. He said believers would lay hands on the sick, he didn't say Pharisees who think they are perfect will perform miracles. I'm pretty sure none of us will attain perfection as long as we live in these bodies, so there's really no reason to think about it. But a lot of people who want to do more for God use the excuse that they have to get a few things worked out first. Don't fall into that trap, God wants to use you, and he wants to use you now!

There is so much more that can be discussed, and so much has already been written about this subject, but I think it can be summed up with a simple statement. Partnering with God is the greatest thing anyone could ever do. There is no higher calling, and there is no better occupation. Have you ever had a job that was so much fun that you jumped out of bed every morning excited that you get to go to work? I doubt many of us have, but that's what this is like. It's so great because it's not really work. The work has already been done. It's like play time. It's like running around on the playground during recess. It really is that much fun. I want to repeat something I said earlier; you are the light of the world, you are the salt of the earth, you are seated with Christ in heavenly places. That's your position. It's something we all need to wrap our heads around because that is how God sees us. There is so much more we could be doing, but we have allowed convenience, and comfort to dictate how much we are willing to do. Here's a news flash for you, serving God is rarely convenient, or comfortable. It requires us to step out of our comfort zones, and take actions that we normally would avoid. Approaching a stranger on the street, and starting a conversation about miracles isn't comfortable. At least it isn't comfortable the first few times. And it certainly doesn't feel good when God lets you feel someone else's pain, so you know what he is getting ready to heal. God rarely waits for us to make some time available to help out. Opportune moments usually pop up at inopportune times. I don't know how many times I have been in a rush to get something finished only to have to pause what I am doing because God showed up, and needed me to do something else. But every bit of it is worth it. I gladly welcome the inconveniences of God. I'd rather have him wake me up at 3 A.M. to have a conversation than to receive a 3 A.M. phone call from work with a problem no one knows how to fix.

It's not just a ministry, it's a lifestyle. We were made to be naturally supernatural in every part of life so this isn't something that needs to be contained within the walls of the church. If anything, the church should be doing a lot more work outside of the walls than inside.

Miracles draw attention, and when the unsaved see what God is doing it is impossible for them to deny his existence. In fact miracles played a large role in conversions during in the early church. When Peter told the lame man to walk in Acts 3^5 it drew a crowd, and gave Peter a perfect opportunity to preach a message. The miracle created an opportunity to share the rest of the story, and in the next chapter we see that many people believed on that day. That's just from one miracle. How would your city respond to seeing miracles every day? I know one thing; it's not something that can be ignored. There are so many people who need to be touched by God. Cities all over the world are literally filled with prayer targets. Some churches have a strong missions focus, and are really concerned about helping those in need. I love those types of churches, and it's one of the major reasons why I attend church where I do because I believe they have grabbed hold of the heart of God. God's heart is to fix all the problems. There are no problems in his kingdom. There is no sickness, sadness, homelessness, hunger, or pain in his kingdom. And there doesn't need to be any here either. Feeding the homeless is awesome, but I like to get them a meal, and a healing. That's the ultimate happy meal, and it is way more fun! Every Christian has the ability, and the mandate to go give people miracles. There are a lot of hurting people in the world, and we hold the answer to their problems. We have a lot of work to do, so stop reading, and get out there!

Endnotes
1. Matthew 11:12
2. Matthew 7:7
3. Matthew 10:8
4. Genesis 3:4-5
5. Acts 3:11

NORMAL

IMPARTATION

In the book of Numbers[1] while the Israelites were traveling to the promised land Moses became a little overwhelmed with leading, so many people, and when he cried out for help, God presented an interesting solution. He told Moses that he would take some of the power of the Spirit that rested on Moses, and distribute it to 70 elders from the tribes. This was the first mention of impartation in the Bible, and later in the New Testament we see Paul mention this concept of impartation on several occasions. He tells the Roman believers that he wants to come see them, so he could impart a spiritual gift that would make them strong[2]. We also see in Acts[3] that the Holy Spirit fell when Peter, and John laid their hands on the people. There is something about praying for others to receive what God has given you that stirs up new spiritual gifts within a person. Paul instructed Timothy to stir up the gifts of God that were in him as a result of the laying on of hands[4].

We have prayed impartation prayers over people, and watched God escalate the works of the Holy Spirit within them in much greater ways than they had previously been used. Now humans cannot give spiritual gifts, that's the job of the Holy Spirit.[5] But the Holy Spirit also does not want these gifts to be locked up in just a few believers. Just as he used Moses, Paul, Pater, and John, he continues to use leaders today to stir up, and impart spiritual gifts so that others can be used in the full capacity for which they were created. My wife and I have received great breakthroughs, and increases in the gifts of the Spirit through impartation, and it is a great joy to impart what I have received to anyone else who want is. So I would like to end this book with a prayer of impartation for you.

Jesus I thank you for all that you have done in, and through me, and I thank you for the awesome privilege, and opportunity to carry your presence, and steward the gifts that you have given to me. I pray that you would impart everything you have given to me to the readers of this book. Just as you took from what was on Moses, I pray that you would also take from what you have placed on me, and release it into their lives today. I ask for a complete transference of the anointing to rest upon them in a mighty way, so that they can be used to bring your kingdom to earth with signs, and wonders following them everywhere they go. Let the sick be healed, lives be restored, and demons run, and hide when they show up, so that you would receive everything you paid for on the cross.

Endnotes
1. Numbers 11:16-17
2. Romans 1:11-12
3. Acts 8:17-18
4. 2 Timothy 1:6 (NKJV)
5. 1 Corinthians 12:11

ABOUT GENE LLOYD

Dr. Gene Lloyd is a twenty year veteran of the U.S. Air Force, a computer scientist, and a second generation minister. He became a full time missionary to Washington D.C. in 2013 after retiring from his Air Force career when he, and his wife Lauren, co-founded Wounded No More, and joined the Apostolic Network of Global Awakening. Their mission is to serve the unmet spiritual and secular needs of the people they minister to, and to teach other believers to do the same. This is accomplished through the supernatural healing of physical, emotional, and spiritual wounds, blended with employment and entrepreneurship training. Gene's writing, and teaching, is a reflection of his passion to change the way the world views God, lead people to understand the depth of God's love, and equip believers to access everything Jesus has made available, so that they can walk in the identity, and authority for which they were created. You can follow their work and ministry at www.facebook.com/woundednomore, Twitter handle @genelloyd, and at www.nomorewounds.org

www.ingramcontent.com/pod-product-compliance
Lightning Source LLC
LaVergne TN
LVHW041542070426
835507LV00011B/884